THE ULTIMATE GUIDE TO
WILD FLOWERS
OF NORTH AMERICA

THE ULTIMATE GUIDE TO
WILD FLOWERS
OF NORTH AMERICA

Joan Barker

Bath • New York • Singapore • Hong Kong • Cologne • Delhi
Melbourne • Amsterdam • Johannesburg • Auckland • Shenzhen

This edition published by Parragon in 2011

Parragon Publishing
Queen Street House
4 Queen Street
Bath, BA1 1HE, UK

Produced by Atlantic Publishing

Photographs courtesy of
Photolibrary.com
(see page 256 for copyright details)
Text © Parragon Books Ltd 2006

ISBN 978-1-4454-3420-9

Printed in China

CONTENTS

INTRODUCTION

ildflowers are flowering plants that grow naturally in the wild – and not just in the open countryside but also in the most urban areas, on vacant lots and cracks in the sidewalk. It is often amazing how such plants will thrive, when all the odds seem to be stacked against them. There is a fine line between weed and wildflower – one person's attractive plant can quite easily be another person's troublesome weed. This book covers the most common wildflowers of North America, but avoids those species that are widely considered to be invasive weeds. However, there are also many plants commonly seen across the continent that are usually thought of as American wildflowers, but which were actually introduced from other areas of the world and have since run wild. Although many of these have been excluded from this book, a few of the most well-loved and widespread are included, along with a note of where they originate from.

The importance of wildflowers

Wildflowers were once thought to be of little practical importance, and they were picked or dug up at will, wiped out in land development schemes or sprayed out of existence on agricultural land. As a result, some have vanished forever, and others are now endangered species. Luckily we are much wiser now, and Congress or local state laws often protect plants that are considered to be at risk. These days it is recognized that many old herbal remedies do have some value – and who knows what valuable natural assets and cures for disease will be discovered as we continue to examine the wildflowers of our planet? It is therefore important to be responsible in the field – make sure to check local laws and never pick a flower or remove a plant from its environment unless you are quite sure it is acceptable to do so.

Plant types

Plants come in three basic types: annuals, biennials and perennials. Annuals flower and die in one season, biennials flower and die in their second year, and perennials live and flower for three or more years. Some biennials and perennials may retain their leaves over the winter; others lose their leaves in the fall, and are classified as herbaceous or deciduous.

Some types keep a few leaves over winter and are described as being semi-evergreen. There is no hard and fast rule as to why some are herbaceous and others evergreen, as both categories can usually be found in members of the same genus.

Plant names

The plant world as a whole is classified into flowering plants (Angiospermae), cone-bearers (Gymno-spermae), and ferns (Pteridophytae). Beyond that plants are divided into families, such as Liliaceae or Fabaceae. Within any given family are to be found genera, such as the genus *Primula* or the genus *Drosera* – the title of the genus is placed in italics, and given a capital letter. Finally, within any given genus are to be found the species, which have a lot in common, can interbreed (hybridize) and often have a limited geographical range; an example is *Drosera rotundifolia* (sundew with round leaves) or *Lilium canadense* (lily from Canada). The specific name is not given a capital letter, but is placed in italics, and it usually has some meaning with regard to the nature or the origin of the plant. Further subdivisions within a given species are indicated by "ssp" meaning "subspecies" or "var." meaning "variety," in that descending order. These abbreviations are not put in italics, so there are some plants with quite complex scientific names, such as *Dichelostemma capitatum* ssp. *capitatum*, or *Thalictrum fendleri* var. *polycarpum*. Wildflowers are often more usually known by their common name, for instance *Lilium canadense* is known as the Canada Lily or Meadow Lily. The plants in this book are listed by the most widely accepted common name for ease of reference, but alternative common names, the scientific name and family of each is also given, to aid in a firm identification. Across the world, the same plant may have many different common names, but the scientific name remains constant. The indexes cover both common and scientific names.

Identifying a wildflower

Whereas cultivated flowers quite often come in a range of colors, each species of wildflower tends to have flowers in only one color, or in a limited range within the color spectrum. The flower can therefore be a very good identifying clue so plants in this book are arranged in color groups.

After color you can also consider the general look of the plant. The type of flower is important – single, spike, cluster. See page 20 for illustrations of each flower type. The shape of the leaves and how they are arranged on the stem can also be a great help in narrowing the choice of potential species. Details of these are given for each entry in the fact box — see the drawings on pages 21–23 for a visual reference for each type.

Having established the flower color of a particular wildflower, look at the habitat it is growing in. North America has a wide range of habitats, from semi-tropical to windswept tundra, from desert and arid grassland to lush and moist woodlands. Forest plants tend to like shade, so will not usually thrive in open meadows; bog plants need a constant supply of water, so will not like areas that dry out on a regular basis. The preferred habitat for all plants is given in the fact box. Some plants can quickly be identified by habitat as they will only grow in a particular conditions, but there are a few that will grow in several types of location, or you may come upon an area that varies in environmental factors in different seasons, and for these the habitat can only be a general guide.

Finally, when you have a general idea of which plant you are looking at, check the range maps and the general description to confirm your identification.

Items of interest

The general text on each plant gives a clear description, information on its uses — both practical and in folklore — and any legends or facts associated with it. Some are noted as poisonous, but this is not an infallible guide. **Do not eat any wild plant unless an expert has confirmed it is safe to do so. Likewise, traditional potions and recipes are referred to throughout the text but readers should consult an expert before experimenting with these.** If a plant is rare, protected or endangered, this is also noted in the text. In general, scientific terms have been avoided, but an explanation of the more common botanical terms is given in the Glossary on pages 14–19.

Good conservation practice

Wildflowers are an essential part of nature, and they also beautify and enrich our environment. Studying them and being able to identify them gives a great deal of pleasure to many people all around the globe. If you do find something in the wild that you cannot identify, or which you think may be rare, draw, or photograph it to take for expert identification. Respect each plant's right to grow where it will, and our world will be a better place for it.

GLOSSARY AND ILLUSTRATIONS

GLOSSARY

Entries marked * are illustrated on pages 20–23

alternate leaf* — leaves arranged alternately up the stem.

anemoniform — flower similar to an anemone.

annual — a plant that flowers and dies in one season.

arrow-shaped leaf* — a leaf with a pointed apex and two pointed lower lobes.

basal — forming or belonging to the bottom layer or base.

basal rosette* — leaves arranged around the base of the stem, to form a rosette.

biennial — a plant that flowers and dies in its second year.

bipinnate leaf* — a compound leaf made up of several pinnate units.

blade — expanded area on either side of the midrib of a leaf.

bracts — specialized leaves that are often brightly colored and resemble a flower.

bulb — swollen underground stem, in which energy is stored to help survive the winter.

calyx — the set of sepals on the base of the flower that protect the flower bud.

carpel — the female reproductive organ of a flower.

clasping leaf*— leaf with its base partly surrounding the stem.

compound leaf — leaf composed of several separate leaflets arising from the same petiole.

compound palmate leaf* — leaf composed of several leaflets to create a palmate shape.

compound pinnate leaf* — leaf composed of several leaflets to create a pinnate shape.

cordate leaf* — a heart–shaped leaf, broadly ovate but with a pointed apex and the base turning in to form a notch for the petiole.

corm — a swollen underground stem, in which energy is stored to help survive the winter.

corymb* — a cluster of florets in which the stalks are arranged at random along the peduncle, but the florets are at one level creating a flat, round top.

cyme* — a cluster of florets in which the inner or top florets open first, blooming downward along the peduncle.

dicotyledon — flowering plant in which the seedling has two leaflets.

dioecious — species in which the stamens and pistils are on separate plants, so plants of both sexes are required before fruit can form.

disk florets — a small, tubular floret, that combines with many others in a disk shape in a composite flower such as a tansy.

elliptical leaf* — a leaf two or three times longer than wide, and tapering to an acute or rounded base.

entire leaf* — leaf with smooth edges.

epiphyte — a plant that grows on another plant.

evergreen — a plant that retains its leaves all year round.

fibrous-rooted — root system made up of main roots branching off into smaller rootlets.

floret — small flower making up a composite flower head.

helicoid cyme* — a cluster of florets, which are all on one side of the peduncle.

herbaceous — a plant that loses its leaves or dies back in the fall.

hermaphroditic — a plant having stamens and pistils in the same flower.

incised leaf* – leaf with deep notches.

indusium – a thin membranous covering.

inflorescence – a cluster of flowers on a floral stem.

involucre – a whorl or rosette of bracts surrounding an inflorescence or at the base of an umbel.

keel – a prow-shaped pair of petals.

lanceolate leaf* – a leaf longer than wide, tapering towards the apex and rounded at the base.

lance-shaped leaf* – a long, pointed leaf, slightly wider at the base but tapering sharply.

linear leaf* – a narrow leaf, several times longer than wide and approximately the same width down its length.

lobed leaf* – leaf with indented edges, with the indents not reaching the center of the blade.

monocarpic – a plant that dies after flowering.

monocotyledon – flowering plant in which the seedling has one leaflet.

monoecious – plants that have male and female flowers on one plant.

net-veined leaf* – leaf in which the veins branch from the main midrib(s) and then subdivide into smaller veinlets.

oblanceolate leaf* – a leaf longer than wide, tapering towards the apex and base.

oblong leaf* – a leaf that is longer than it is wide, with a roughly even width along most of its length and rounded at both base and apex.

obovate leaf* – an egg–shaped leaf, wide at the apex and tapering towards the base.

opposite leaf* – leaves arrange opposite each other along the stem.

orbicular leaf* – a rounded, circular leaf.

ovate leaf* – an egg-shaped leaf, wide at the base and tapering toward the apex.

palmate leaf* – leaf with five or more lobes whose midribs all radiate from one point.

panicle – a loose, branching cluster of flowers.

parallel-veined leaf* – leaf in which the veins run essentially parallel to each other, connected by minute, straight veinlets.

peduncle – an elongated flower stem.

pendent – hanging down.

perennial – a plant that lives and flowers for three or more years.

perfect flower – a flower that contains functional stamens and pistils.

perfoliate leaf* – leaf with the stem piercing it.

petals – the highly colored portions of a flower.

petiole – stalk that supports the leaf blade.

pinna – primary division of a pinnate leaf, especially a fern (plural pinnae).

pinnate leaf* – compound leaf with pairs of leaflets arranged alternately on either side of the stem.

pinnatifid – divided pinnately, but not all the way to the central axis.

pseudoumbels – looking like umbels.

raceme* – flower cluster with separate flowers attached by short, equal stalks at equal distances along a central stem.

ray florets – a strap-shaped floret, that combines with many others in a ray formation in a composite flower such as a dandelion.

remontant – plant that will flower a second time if dead-headed.

reniform – kidney-shaped.

rhizomes – swollen underground stem, in which energy is stored to help survive the winter.

rhomboidal leaf* – a leaf in a rhomboid shape, wide in the center and tapering sharply at apex and base.

scandent — having a climbing habit.

scorpioid cyme* — a cluster of florets, which are alternate to each other along the peduncle.

semi-evergreen — a plant that retains a few leaves over the winter.

sepals — small, green, leaf-like structures on the base of the flower that protect the flower bud.

serrated leaf* — leaf with saw teeth pointing towards the apex.

sessile — attached directly by its base, without a stalk or peduncle.

simple leaf — leaf in which the blade is a single continuous unit.

solitary flower — a single flower on a stem.

sorus — spore-producing receptacle on the underside of a fern frond (plural sori).

spadix — a spike of minute flowers closely arranged round a fleshy axis, and typically enclosed in a spathe.

spathe — large sheathing bract enclosing the flower cluster.

spatulate leaf* — a rounded leaf, tapering towards the base.

spike* — flower cluster with separate sessile flowers, at equal distances along a central stem.

sporangium — receptacle in which asexual spores are formed (plural sporangia).

spore — a reproductive cell.

spur — a slender, tubular projection from the base of a flower.

stipule — a small, leaf-like appendage to a leaf, typically in pairs at the base of the leaf stalk.

stolon — a creeping horizontal plant stem or runner, that takes root along its length to form new plants.

tepal — a segment of the outer whorl of a flower that has no difference between petals and sepals.

terrestrial — on the ground.

toothed leaf* — leaf with notched edges.

tripalmate leaf* — leaf formed of three leaflets in a palmate shape.

tuber — swollen underground stem, in which energy is stored to help survive the winter.

twining — twisting around.

umbel* — a cluster of florets in which the stalks arise from one point, but the florets are at one level creating a flat, round top.

whorled leaf* — leaves arranged in circles along the stem.

Flowers

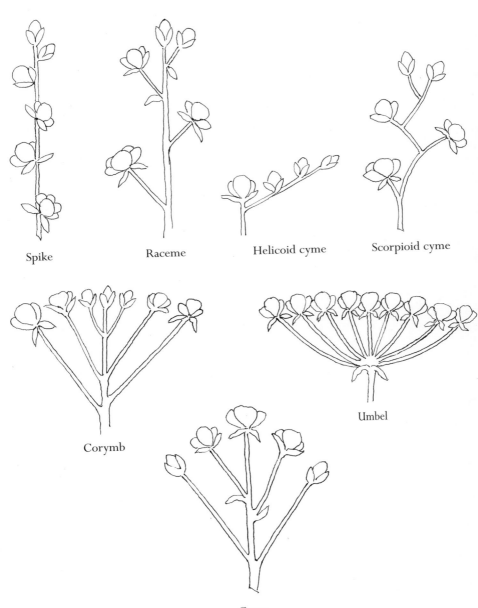

Spike

Raceme

Helicoid cyme

Scorpioid cyme

Corymb

Umbel

Cyme

Leaves

Lanceolate

Oblanceolate

Spatulate

Orbicular

Oblong

Elliptical

Ovate

Obovate

Basal rosette

Tripalmate

Arrow-shaped

Rhomboidal

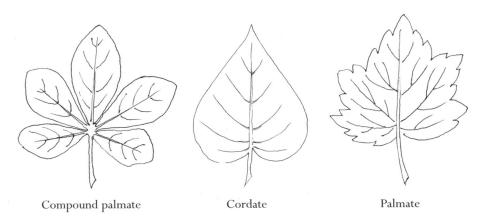

Compound palmate   Cordate   Palmate

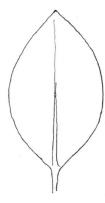

Lance-shaped   Perfoliate leaf   Clasping leaf   Entire

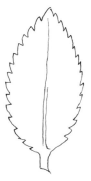

Serrated   Lobed   Incised   Toothed

Whorled

Alternated

Opposite

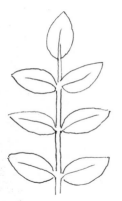

Pinnate

Compound pinnate

Bipinnate

Parallel veined

Linear

Net veined

SCARLET PIMPERNEL; POOR MAN'S WEATHERGLASS

(ANAGALLIS ARVENSIS)

The Scarlet Pimpernel is a plant that originates from Europe, but it is now found across much of North America. Its European name of Poor Man's Weatherglass was given because the flowers open only when the sun is shining, closing when the weather is either overcast or wet. Scarlet Pimpernel is an annual and creeps across the ground. Its flowers are borne on long, slim stalks springing from the axil of each bright green leaf and are usually bright red or a vivid red-orange, although there are also blue and white varieties, which are both rare. This plant looks extremely attractive, and may seem like a very good addition to a wildflower garden, but it is also poisonous and can cause dermatitis.

FAMILY Primrose
DESCRIPTION Creeping, low-growing plant with a star-shaped flower on a long stalk
HABITAT Roadsides; waste ground; garden lawns
HEIGHT 4–12 ins (10–30 cm)
FLOWER Radially symmetrical, $\frac{1}{4}$ in (0.60 cm) in diameter
FLOWERING June–August
LEAVES Ovate, $\frac{1}{4}$–$1\frac{1}{4}$ ins (0.60–3 cm) long, opposite, no stalk

GIANT RED PAINTBRUSH
(CASTILLEJA MINIATA)

FAMILY Figwort

DESCRIPTION Leafy plant with an elongated flower cluster that looks like a ragged paintbrush

HABITAT Mountain meadows; forest clearings

HEIGHT 12–38 ins (30–95 cm)

FLOWER Elongated cluster, each flower ½–1½ ins (1.25–3.75 cm) long

FLOWERING May–August

LEAVES Narrowly lanceolate, up to 4 ins (10 cm) long

It is easy to see how Giant Red Paintbrush gets its common name – its flower resembles a rather ragged paintbrush that has been dipped in bright red paint. It is a fairly tall plant with a single stem bearing many narrowly lanceolate alternate leaves, the upper ones either smooth or covered in slightly sticky hairs. At the tip of the stem is an elongated rounded cluster of bright crimson, tubular flowers with four pointed lobes. The brightly colored bracts beneath are usually red, but may very occasionally be yellow or orange. There are around 109 species in this genus found in North America, most of them in the east.

ROSY PAINTBRUSH
(CASTILLEJA RHEXIFOLIA)

Rosy Paintbrush is an erect and leafy plant, with long, lanceolate leaves arranged alternately. It has brightly colored bracts surrounding the flowers, which are more conspicuous than the flowers themselves. Great Plains Paintbrush, or Downy Painted Cup (*C. miniata*), has multiple, hairy stems clustered together, with long, narrow lower leaves and upper leaves often with three to five rather narrow lobes. The flowers are yellow-pink, long and sickle-shaped, with a very protruding curved corolla and yellow to pink bracts. Many species of *Castilleja* are difficult to transplant, because they are partially parasitic on neighboring plants.

FAMILY Figwort

DESCRIPTION Erect and leafy plant, with bright red bracts surrounding the flower at the top of the stem

HABITAT Fields; moist meadows

HEIGHT 5–20 ins (12–50 cm)

FLOWER Elongated terminal cluster, with each flower ½–1½ ins (1.25–3.75 cm) in length

FLOWERING June–September

LEAVES Lanceolate, 1–3 ins (2.5–7.5 cm) in length

CALIFORNIA POPPY
(ESCHSCHOLZIA CALIFORNICA)

The California Poppy grows abundantly in the wild in the valleys and foothills of the Pacific coast and in parts of the Rockies, but is also a very popular ornamental plant. It has several blue-green stems and deeply dissected, rather fern-like blue-green leaves. The bright-colored flower is held on the end of a long, bare stalk and is usually a simple bright orange, but may range from yellow-orange to a deep orange, or even have petals that grade in color from orange at the base to yellow at the tips. The flowers open only in very bright sunlight, closing at night and on very overcast days. The California Poppy has been the state flower of California since 1903. The very similar Mexican Gold Poppy (*Eschscholtzia californica* ssp *mexicana* – see page 40), which is a sub-species of the California Poppy, has more orange flowers and is found in the southeast and the south.

FAMILY Poppy

DESCRIPTION Blue-green plant with several smooth stems, feathery leaves, open red-orange colored flowers, each on a single long stalk

HABITAT Open meadows; grassy hillsides

HEIGHT 9–26 ins (22–65 cm)

FLOWER Radially symmetrical, 1–2 ins (2.5–5 cm) in diameter

FLOWERING February–September

LEAVES Bipinnate, finely dissected, with long stalks

CARDINAL FLOWER
(LOBELIA CARDINALIS)

FAMILY Bellflower

DESCRIPTION Erect plant with clusters of leafy stems and spikes of red flowers

HABITAT Damp areas beside streams

HEIGHT 12–48 ins (60–120 cm)

FLOWER Tall spike, each bilaterally symmetrical flower up to 1½ in (3.75 cm) long

FLOWERING July–September

LEAVES Oval to lanceolate, finely toothed, 2–5 ins (5–12.5 cm) long

Cardinal Flower is a tall, leafy perennial, with bright red, tubular flowers arranged along the stem in a tall spike. The length of the flowers and their bright red color means they are usually pollinated by hummingbirds, which feed on the nectar. Although this species is quite common, its showy flowers mean they are often picked, which has made it scarce in some areas of its range. The alternate leaves are long, oval to lanceolate, and toothed. American Indians used a tea made from the roots for stomach-ache and typhoid, and made a leaf tea for colds, headaches, and rheumatism. However, Cardinal Flower is considered potentially poisonous.

GOLDEN-BEARD PENSTEMON
(PENSTEMON BARBATUS)

Golden-beard Penstemon gets its rather unusual name from a small tuft of bright yellow hairs that protrude beyond the long stamens, through the flower opening. The bright scarlet flowers are long and irregular, with two symmetrical halves, and droop from short stalks that spring from the upper leaf axils. They form a long, loose cluster at the top of the plant. Golden-beard Penstemon is tall and slender, with only a few long and narrow, smooth, gray-green leaves, which are arranged in opposite pairs along the upright stem. It prefers to grow on dry, rocky slopes in open forested areas.

FAMILY Figwort
DESCRIPTION Tall plant with sparse gray-green leaves and slender red flowers held in a long cluster
HABITAT Dry, rocky slopes
HEIGHT 26–36 ins (65–90 cm)
FLOWER Elongated cluster, each flower 1–1½ ins (2.5–3.75 cm) long
FLOWERING July–September
LEAVES Narrow, 2–5 ins (5–12.5 cm) long, arranged in opposite pairs

ROCK PENSTEMON; CLIFF PENSTEMON (PENSTEMON RUPICOLA)

FAMILY Figwort
DESCRIPTION Mat-forming plant, with many bright red-pink tubular flowers in racemes
HABITAT Rock ledges and slopes
HEIGHT Creeper, 6 ins (15 cm)
FLOWER Tubular, with two symmetrical halves, 1–1½ ins (2.5–3.75 cm) in length
FLOWERING June–August
LEAVES Ovate, thick, irregularly toothed, ½–1 in (1.5–2.5 cm) long

Rock Penstemon grows on rock ledges, rocky slopes, and cliffs. It is a low-growing creeper, with reclining stems bearing many long, ovate, thick leaves. These have small, irregular teeth and are arranged closely together in opposite pairs. As the plant spreads, it forms a thick mat over the ground. The bright red or rose-pink flowers are tubular, with two symmetrical halves, and are clustered together on short, upright stems in a dense raceme cluster. As there are usually many flower stalks very close together, the plant forms a bright carpet of color over the ground when it is in bloom.

INDIAN PINK
(SILENE CALIFORNICA)

As its scientific name suggests, Indian Pink is mainly found in California, and although it is quite widespread within its limited range it is by no means that common. It is a medium-sized plant with leafy and branching stems that are sometimes trailing, sometimes erect. The bright green leaves are ovate, quite long and arranged in opposite pairs. The flowers have five broad, open petals that are deeply notched at the tips and are bright red in color. They are borne at the ends of the stems, usually those that are more erect. There are around 30 species within this genus found in North America, and these are spread across the continent.

FAMILY Carnation
DESCRIPTION Trailing, leafy plant with bright red pinwheel flowers at the ends of stems
HABITAT Dry, rocky woodland
HEIGHT 8–18 ins (20–45 cm)
FLOWER Radially symmetrical, 1–1½ ins (2.5–3.75 cm) in diameter
FLOWERING May–July
LEAVES Ovate, 1¼ –3 ins (3–7.5 cm), arranged in opposite pairs

FIRE PINK
(SILENE VIRGINICA)

A fairly tall plant, Fire Pink has leafy, slender, and branching stems, some of which are erect and some trailing. The spatulate to lanceolate basal leaves are bright green, while those on the stem itself are comparatively long, sessile, and arranged in opposite pairs. The bright red flowers have five narrow, open petals that are deeply divided at the tips, and sepals that are joined to form a tube. They are borne in loose clusters at the ends of the stems. Fire Pink resembles Indian Pink (*S. californica* – see page 33) but is found in eastern North America and not in the west. Another western plant, Cardinal Catchfly (*S. laciniata*), is also very similar to both but it has erect stems and is slightly taller.

FAMILY Carnation

DESCRIPTION Slender-stemmed plant, often trailing, with bright red pinwheel flowers on long stalks

HABITAT Dry, sandy woodland

HEIGHT 8–30 ins (20–75 cm)

FLOWER Radially symmetrical, 1½ ins (3.75 cm) in diameter

FLOWERING April–July

LEAVES Basal, spatulate or lanceolate, 1½–4 ins (4–10 cms), stem leaves 6 ins (15 cm) long in opposite pairs with no stalk

PURPLE TRILLIUM; STINKING BENJAMIN; WAKEROBIN (TRILLIUM ERECTUM)

FAMILY Lily

DESCRIPTION Nodding red-brown flower on a long stalk above a whorl of diamond-shaped leaves

HABITAT Woodland

HEIGHT 8–16 ins (20–40 cm)

FLOWER Radially symmetrical, 2½ ins (6.25 cm) in diameter

FLOWERING April–June

LEAVES Diamond-shaped, up to 7 ins (17.5 cm) long, dark green, with a very short stalk

Although the flower of Purple Trillium looks very attractive, unfortunately it smells extremely unpleasant; the stink attracts carrion flies for pollination. Its alternative name of Stinking Benjamin is therefore quite descriptive. The flower is a deep red-brown to maroon in color rather than purple and has three pointed petals alternating with three sepals. It is borne at the end of a rather drooping stalk that springs from the center of a whorl of three dark green, diamond-shaped to ovate leaves. American Indians once used the root medicinally as an aid during childbirth, and to treat the problems arising during the menopause.

INDIAN PINK; PINK-ROOT
(SPIGELIA MARILANDICA)

As well as growing in the wild, Indian Pink also does well when cultivated so it is sometimes included in wildflower gardens. It is distinctive in appearance as it has unusual trumpet-shaped flowers, which are a deep, bright red on the outside and creamy-yellow on the inside. They are held in a narrow, one-sided terminal cluster, and the plant flowers from the bottom of the cluster upwards. The tall stem bears opposite pairs of long, sessile leaves that are ovate or broadly lanceolate in shape. American Indians and early physicians used the plant to treat worms, especially in young children, but in some cases it can have quite serious and unpleasant side effects.

FAMILY Logania

DESCRIPTION Leafy plant with distinctive trumpet-shaped flowers, red outside and yellow inside

HABITAT Damp woodland

HEIGHT 12–24 ins (30–60 cm)

FLOWER Trumpet-shaped, 1 in (2.5 cm) in length

FLOWERING May–June

LEAVES Narrowly ovate, sessile, 2–4 ins (5–10 cm) long, arranged opposite

ORANGE MILKWEED; BUTTERFLY WEED; PLEURISY ROOT

(ASCLEPIAS TUBEROSA)

Although Orange Milkweed is part of the Milkweed family, its leafy and hairy stem bears alternate leaves – the only Milkweed to do so – and the leaves have a clear sap, rather than a milky-colored one. The plant is noticeable for its spectacular clusters of bright orange flowers, which attract many passing butterflies. This accounts for the common name of Butterfly Weed, while Pleurisy Root comes from the plant having been used to treat pleurisy and other lung problems by early physicians. It prefers dry places, particularly prairies but also brush or open woodland. Although it is such an attractive plant, and despite having been voted the fourth most showy wildflower, it is not generally cultivated in gardens.

FAMILY Milkweed
DESCRIPTION Leafy, hairy-stemmed plant with umbel cluster of orange flowers at the top of the stem
HABITAT Roadsides; fields
HEIGHT 12–18 ins (30–45 cm)
FLOWER Umbel cluster, 2 ins (5 cm) in width
FLOWERING June–August
LEAVES Lance-shaped, narrow, 2–6 ins (5–15 cm) long, arranged alternately on stem

MEXICAN GOLD POPPY
(ESCHSCHOLZIA CALIFORNICA SSP. MEXICANA)

FAMILY Poppy

DESCRIPTION Blue-green, smooth-stemmed plant, with fern-like leaves at the base and orange-yellow flowers on a long stalk

HABITAT Gravelly desert

HEIGHT 10–18 ins (25–45 cm)

FLOWER Radially symmetrical, ¾–2 ins (2–5 cm) in diameter

FLOWERING March–June

LEAVES Bipinnate, finely dissected, ¾–2 ins (2–5 cm) long

Although it was once considered to be a species in its own right, Mexican Gold Poppy is now generally considered to be a sub-species of California Poppy (*E. californica* — see pages 28–9). The several blue-green stems bear deeply dissected, rather fern-like leaves towards the base and a bright flower on the end of a long, bare stalk. The bowl-shaped flowers only open in sunlight, closing at night and on very cloudy days. They have four broad orange-yellow petals, often grading in color from deep orange at the base to pale yellow or cream at the tips. There are around ten species in this genus found in western North America.

ORANGE JEWELWEED; SPOTTED TOUCH-ME-NOT
(IMPATIENS CAPENSIS)

There are 10 species of Jewelweed in North America, most of which prefer wet ground. Orange Jewelweed is an annual with a branched stem, alternate, long, thinly ovate and bluntly toothed leaves. The bright orange flowers spotted with red-brown are borne on drooping stems, and have a spur at the back that curls round and underneath. Its alternate name of Touch-me-not comes from the ripe fruits, which explode when touched. The young shoots can be used as potherbs, and the plant's juice relieves the symptoms of poison ivy. The leaves have been scientifically proven to have both antihistamine and anti-inflammatory properties.

FAMILY Touch-me-not

DESCRIPTION Very tall, leafy plant with orange-yellow flowers splotched with brown

HABITAT Shady wet ground

HEIGHT 3–5 ft (90–150 cm)

FLOWER Irregular, two symmetrical halves, 1 in (2.5 cm) long

FLOWERING June–September

LEAVES Thinly ovate, blunt toothed, 1½–3 ins (4–7.5 cm) long, lower opposite, upper alternate

CANADA LILY; WILD YELLOW LILY; FIELD LILY

(LILIUM CANADENSE)

The Canada Lily is not particularly well-named, since it is found not only in Canada but also in the eastern states of the United States and west across Arkansas, Kansas, and Nebraska. Its tall stem bears long, lanceolate leaves arranged in whorls, and showy, nodding, bell-shaped flowers, which can be orange, red-orange, or yellow, with dark spots. There are usually a large number of flowers on each stem – sometimes as many as 20 – either on long stalks springing from the leaf axils or arranged in a cluster at the top of the stem. American Indians traditionally made a tea from the roots of this plant to treat stomach problems, dysentery, and rheumatism, and also applied a poultice of the roots to snakebites.

FAMILY Lily

DESCRIPTION Tall stem with whorled leaves, with one or several nodding orange to yellow flowers on separate stalks at the top of the plant

HABITAT Wet meadows; edges of damp woodland

HEIGHT 2–5 ft (60–150 cm)

FLOWER Bell-shaped, 2–3 ins (5–8 cm) in diameter

FLOWERING June–August

LEAVES Lanceloate, 6 ins (15 cm) long, whorled

SCARLET GLOBE-MALLOW;
RED FALSE MALLOW (SPHAERALCEA COCCINEA)

FAMILY Mallow
DESCRIPTION Leafy, branching plant, with velvety hairs and narrow clusters of orange-red flowers
HABITAT Arid, open ground
HEIGHT 18–22 ins (45–55 cm)
FLOWER Radially symmetrical, 1–1½ ins (2.5–3.75 cm) in diameter
FLOWERING May–August
LEAVES Orbicular, palmately dissected, with toothed lobes, ½–2 ins (1.25–5 cm) across

Scarlet Globe-mallow is a leafy, branching, velvet-haired plant, with almost round, palmately dissected, irregularly toothed leaves. The flowers are orange to orange-red, and are borne in narrow clusters springing from the upper leaf axils. It is fairly easy to recognize as a species because of its bright orange flowers with their five broad petals, which are unusual in its range. However, it may be more difficult to identify it precisely, as there are many other, very similar species of globe-mallow within the same general area. Scaly Globe-mallow (*S. leptophylla*) shares the same range in the south and has gray hairs that are more like scales.

SWEETFLAG
(ACORUS CALAMUS)

There are two species of Sweetflag in North America, one native and the other introduced from Eurasia, but they are almost impossible to tell apart, to the extent that some authorities class them as the same species. The long, narrow, linear leaves spring from a thick rhizome and are parallel-veined. The flower spike consists of many densely-clustered yellow flowers arranged in a diamond pattern and sticks out at an angle around halfway up a stalk that otherwise looks like another leaf. Young rhizomes can be eaten raw or added to salads, and American Indians ate the root for stomach problems and as a stimulant on long journeys.

FAMILY Sweetflag

DESCRIPTION Wet habitat plant with long, linear leaves and a jutting spike of yellow-green or brownish flowers

HABITAT Streams; swamps; marshes; along rivers

HEIGHT 12–50 ins (30–125 cm)

FLOWER Spike, each with many tiny flowers $\frac{1}{8}$ in (0.3 cm) long

FLOWERING May–August

LEAVES Linear, parallel-veined, 1–4 ft (30–120 cms) long

GOLDEN COLUMBINE
(AQUILEGIA CHRYSANTHA)

There are 23 species of wild Columbine to be found across North America, but since it is a graceful and attractive wildflower many more have been developed as cultivated garden flowers. Columbine flowers can be yellow, red, cream, pink, or blue – the Colorado Blue Columbine (*A. caerulea* – see pages 236–7), is Colorado's state flower. In the wild, many of the yellow-flowered varieties are now quite rare, to the point that they are officially endangered. Golden Columbine is a branching, bushy perennial with compound palmate leaves and attractive, bright yellow flowers on long stalks. Each of the flower petals has a long spur extending from the back, which makes the flower very distinctive and showy. The plant prefers to grow in moist and sheltered places.

FAMILY Buttercup
DESCRIPTION Bushy plant with several stems, divided leaves and bright yellow flowers on long stalks
HABITAT Damp shade
HEIGHT 16–48 ins (40–120 cm)
FLOWER Radially symmetrical, 1½–3 ins (3.75–8 cm) in diameter
FLOWERING July–August
LEAVES Compound palmate, deeply cleft and lobed, 1½ ins (4 cm) long

BLACK MUSTARD
(BRASSICA NIGRA)

FAMILY Mustard
DESCRIPTION Branching plant with deeply-lobed lower leaves and terminal clusters of small, bright yellow flowers
HABITAT Fields; waste ground
HEIGHT 24–36 ins (60–90 cm)
FLOWER Terminal cluster, each flower ½ in (1.25 cm) in width
FLOWERING June–October
LEAVES Upper, lanceolate, toothed; lower, lanceolate, deeply lobed, 1½–3 ins (4–7.5 cm) long

Black Mustard originates from Europe, but it is now naturalized and very common across most of North America although it is rare in the southeast. It is a widely branching plant, with deeply-lobed, alternate lower leaves, usually with one large terminal lobe and four smaller side ones. The smaller upper leaves are toothed. The flowers are in small clusters at the top of each stem branch. The seeds of Black Mustard are used in pickling recipes and ground for mustard, and are also eaten as a tonic. Brassicas have been scientifically proven to contain strong anti-cancer compounds, but eating large quantities can cause skin blotches and occasionally ulcers.

GREENEYES; CHOCOLATE FLOWER
(BERLANDIERA LYRATA)

There are five species of *Berlandiera* across the United States, but Greeneyes is the most common. It is a tall, leafy, branching plant, with the upper branches sprawling and ending in compound flower heads with yellow rays and a maroon central disk. The flowers may smell of chocolate, hence the alternative common name of Chocolate Flower. The leaves are long and velvety, either with scalloped edges or divided pinnately into segments, which also have scalloped edges. The genus name honors a 19th century French-Swiss physician, Jean-Louis Berlandier, who collected plants across its growing area.

FAMILY Aster

DESCRIPTION Leafy plant with long, velvety alternate leaves and compound flowers with bright yellow rays and a maroon central disk

HABITAT Roadsides; grassy areas on stony soil

HEIGHT 12–48 ins (30–120 cm)

FLOWER Radially symmetrical 1½ ins (3.75 cm) in diameter

FLOWERING May–October

LEAVES Scalloped edges, sometimes pinnately divided

LANCELEAF COREOPSIS;
TICKSEED (COREOPSIS LANCEOLATA)

FAMILY Aster
DESCRIPTION Tall, branching plant with yellow, compound flowers on long stalks, with a yellow central disk
HABITAT Waste ground; roadsides; disturbed and poor soil
HEIGHT 12–24 ins (30–60 cm)
FLOWER Radially symmetrical, 2–3 ins (5–8 cm) in diameter
FLOWERING May–July
LEAVES Lance-shaped; lower more elliptical, 3–6 ins (7.5–15 cm) long; upper unstalked and rather oblong

A native American wildflower that originates in the Midwest, Lanceleaf Coreopsis is now also common across the northeast – probably after having escaped from gardens. It is quite a tall, branching plant, with bright yellow compound flowers at the end of long stalks. The rays have unusual scalloped tips and the central disk is yellow. It is similar to Garden Coreopsis (*C. tinctoria*), which has a maroon central disk and red at the base of the rays; where these species cohabit they hybridize, leading to plants with characteristics of both, as in the picture above. The leaves are broadly lance-shaped, the lower ones elliptical and the upper ones wider and more oblong.

SULFUR BUCKWHEAT
(ERIOGONUM UMBELLATUM)

Sulfur Buckwheat has short, woody branches ending in clusters of long, ovate leaves on slender stalks. These leaves are gray-green in color and have very hairy undersides. The long, bare, erect flower stalks spring from the leaves, bearing tiny yellow-cream or yellow flowers in small, rounded clusters. The flowers grow from tiny cups, with several springing from each – a typical feature of the flowers of this species. There are 180 species in this genus in North America, most found in the western half of the continent.

FAMILY Buckwheat

DESCRIPTION Erect, long-stalked plant with yellow or creamy-yellow flowers in a rounded cluster

HABITAT Sagebrush deserts; dry foothills

HEIGHT 3–16 ins (8–40 cm)

FLOWER Rounded clusters 2–4 ins (5–10 cm) in diameter arranged in an umbel cluster

FLOWERING May–August

LEAVES Ovate, hairy beneath, ½–1½ ins (1.5–4 cm) long, on slender stalks

TROUT LILY;
DOGTOOTH VIOLET
(ERYTHRONIUM AMERICANUM)

One of the most distinctive features of the Trout Lily is its mottled brown leaves, the patterning of which is supposed to resemble that of the Brown Trout fish – hence the flower's common name. The plant has only two leaves, which are long, elliptical to oval, and which sheath the base of the stem. The small but very showy flower is borne at the end of a bare stalk, and is yellow outside but more bronze in color inside, with slightly backward-curving sepals and petals. There may be several flowers on a plant, each with its own stalk. Trout Lily prefers to grow in woodland and meadows. It was once used medicinally in exactly the same way as White Trout Lily (*E. albidum* – see pages 122–3), which has white flowers, often tinged with lavender. There are around 18 species in this genus found across North America.

FAMILY Lily
DESCRIPTION Stalk with one nodding yellow flower, springing from a pair of basal, brown-mottled leaves
HABITAT Woodland; meadows
HEIGHT 4–12 ins (10–30 cm)
FLOWER Radially symmetrical, 1 in (2.5 cm) in diameter
FLOWERING March–May
LEAVES Basal sheath, elliptical, 2–8 ins (2–20 cm) long

YELLOW BELL
(FRITILLARIA PUDICA)

FAMILY Lily

DESCRIPTION Delicate plant with bright green linear leaves and hanging, urn-shaped yellow flowers

HABITAT Grassy meadows; grassland; sagebrush; open forests

HEIGHT 6–12 ins (15–30 cm)

FLOWER Urn-shaped, pendant, ½–1 in (1.25–2.5 cm) in length

FLOWERING March–July

LEAVES Linear, 2–8 ins (5–20 cm) long

Fritillaries are perennials, springing from a small bulb, and there are around 19 different species found across North America. Yellow Bell is a rather charming, delicate-looking plant, with a few linear, bright green leaves arranged near the base of the stem. Each plant bears one, solitary, nodding, urn-shaped yellow flower on a long stalk. The flower is quite long and narrow with six petal-like segments, and turns from yellow to purple-red as it matures and begins to wither away. Yellow Bell is quite common within most of its range, where it grows in meadows, grasslands, and open forests.

CURLYCUP GUMWEED;
(GRINDELIA SQUARROSA) STICKYHEADS

Curlycup Gumweed spreads quickly in heavily grazed areas as its bitter taste ensures livestock avoid it. It is an erect, branching plant with alternate long, oblong, and toothed leaves springing directly from the stem. The leaves are scattered with translucent glands which excrete a strong-smelling substance, possibly to repel leaf-eating insects and animals. The flower heads have pale yellow ray flowers with a darker yellow disk. The pointed bracts at the flower base curl outwards and are sticky, hence the alternative common name of Stickyheads. American Indians made a medicinal tea from the plant, and a leaf poultice for wounds.

FAMILY Aster

DESCRIPTION Small, stout plant with erect stem, several branches with yellow, daisy-like flowers

HABITAT Prairies; waste ground

HEIGHT 6–30 ins (15–75 cm)

FLOWER Compound flower head, 1 in (2.5 cm) in diameter

FLOWERING July–October

LEAVES Oblong, sessile, toothed, 1–2½ ins (2.5–6.5 cm) long, with many translucent spots

SNEEZEWEED
(HELENIUM AUTUMNALE)

The dried leaves of Sneezeweed were once used in snuff, to promote sneezing to rid the body of evil spirits, from which it gets its common name. It was also traditionally used as a folk remedy for fevers. There are 20 species of sneezeweed found across North America, all with yellow ray petals. This species is a tall plant, with a leafy stem ending in a compound flower head. The distinctive ball of disk flowers at the center is surrounded by long, drooping ray petals. As its Latin name implies, Sneezeweed flowers late in the year in latter part of summer or fall. Its leaves are long lanceolate and toothed, and are arranged alternately along the stem, with their bases extending down the stem on either side like tiny wings. Other species of sneezeweed found in North America include Purple-head Sneezeweed (*H. flexuosum*), which has a purple-brown central disk, and Slender-leaved Sneezeweed (*H. amarum*), which has very thin, almost thread-like, leaves.

FAMILY Aster

DESCRIPTION Tall, leafy plant with daisy-like flower heads, the fan-shape rays drooping and the central disk forming a rounded ball

HABITAT Swamps; wet fields; roadsides

HEIGHT 2–6 ft (60–180 cm)

FLOWER Compound flower head, 1–2 ins (2.5–5 cm) in diameter

FLOWERING August–November

LEAVES Lanceolate, coarsely-toothed, sessile, 6 ins (15 cm) long, arranged alternately

COMMON SUNFLOWER
(HELIANTHUS ANNUUS)

FAMILY Aster
DESCRIPTION Tall, leafy plant, with a hairy erect stem, branching at the top and bearing many flower heads with yellow rays and a maroon-brown central disk
HABITAT Dry open fields; roadsides; plains; foothills
HEIGHT 2–13 ft (60–390 cm)
FLOWER Compound flower head, 3–5 ins (7.5–12.5 cm) in diameter
FLOWERING June–September
LEAVES Ovate or heart-shaped, sometimes toothed, 3–12 ins (7.5–30 cm) long; upper leaves a little smaller

The state flower of Kansas, the Common Sunflower is a tall, leafy plant and the bright yellow flower face follows the sun as it moves across the sky. The sunflower has long been cultivated in North America; the seeds are edible and used for cooking oil and livestock fodder, and Native Americans obtained a dull blue dye from the seeds and a yellow dye from the flower heads for use in traditional basketwork and weaving. They also ground sunflower seeds to make bread flour and used the oil to dress hair. In the 19th century, many believed that growing the Common Sunflower near a house would protect the occupants from malaria.

GIANT SUNFLOWER
(HELIANTHUS GIGANTEUS)

The name Giant Sunflower refers to the height of this species, which can be up to seven feet (210 cm), as it does not have a very large flower. The rough, reddish-purple stem, bears long, lanceolate, finely toothed but rough-surfaced leaves, usually arranged alternately, but sometimes opposite. The compound flower head has several bright yellow pointed ray flowers, around a darker yellow central disk. There are around 50 species of native sunflower across North America, most of which grow east of the Rockies. Wild sunflower seeds are very nutritious, and are an important winter food for songbirds and gamebirds.

FAMILY Aster

DESCRIPTION Very tall, rough-stemmed plant, with many light yellow, daisy-like flowers

HABITAT Swamps; wet open ground

HEIGHT 3–7 ft (90–210 cm)

FLOWER Compound flower head, 2–3 ins (5–8 cm) in diameter

FLOWERING July–October

LEAVES Lanceolate, finely-toothed, rough, 3–7 ins (7.5–17.5 cm) long

MAXIMILIAN'S SUNFLOWER
(HELIANTHUS MAXIMILIANII)

A native American wildflower, Maximilian's Sunflower grows across the prairies and is a valuable addition to the diet of livestock, while the seeds are an important food for wildlife. Like other species of sunflower, it has a rough, stout stem that branches near the top and bears alternate, rather widely spaced leaves. These are long, stiff, and narrowly elliptical in shape, and are often folded lengthwise with downward-curving tips. The large yellow flower heads are borne at the end of short stalks springing from the upper half of the plant and are made up of many pointed ray flowers around a fairly small central disk. Maximilian's Sunflower was named after an early nineteenth century naturalist, Prince Maximilian of Wied-Neuwied. Other species of prairie sunflower include Willow-leaved Sunflower (*H. Salicifolious*) with long, narrow, drooping leaves, and Common Sunflower (*H. annuus* – see page 58).

FAMILY Aster
DESCRIPTION Tall plant with yellow daisy-like flowers on rough stems on the upper part of the stalk
HABITAT Prairies
HEIGHT 3–10 ft (90–300 cm)
FLOWER Compound flower head, 2–3 ins (5-7.5 cm) in diameter
FLOWERING July–October
LEAVES Narrowly elliptical, stiff, rough, 4–6 ins (10–15 cm) long, arranged alternately

JERUSALEM ARTICHOKE
(HELIANTHUS TUBEROSUS)

FAMILY Aster

DESCRIPTION Stout, branching plant with rough stems bearing large yellow flower heads

HABITAT Roadside; field edges

HEIGHT 6–10 ft (180–300 cm)

FLOWER Compound flower head, 3 ins (8 cm) in diameter

FLOWERING August–October

LEAVES Lanceolate or ovate, 4–10 ins (10–25 cm) long

Despite its common name, this plant has nothing to do with Jerusalem – it is actually a member of the Aster family like the Sunflower. Jerusalem Artichoke is a perennial with a branching stem bearing opposite lower leaves and alternate upper leaves. The leaves are lanceolate or ovate and rather rough and thick. The plant tends to grow in colonies and was cultivated by American Indians for its tubers, which can be eaten raw or cooked like potatoes but are without starch and very nutritious. Today the Jerusalem Artichoke is sometimes grown as a crop, so its tubers may be found in food markets.

COMMON ST.-JOHN'S-WORT
(HYPERICUM PERFORATUM)

A European wildflower, Common St.-John's-Wort was introduced to North America and is now found in abundance across much of the continent, to the point where it is considered a weed in some states. Its branching, bushy stem has small, long, elliptical leaves and each branch ends in a small cluster of bright yellow flowers, which have tiny black dots on the edges of the petals. St.-John's-Wort is one of the best-known and popular herbal remedies for mild depression, but eating the raw plant can cause photodermatitis in both cattle and humans.

FAMILY St.-John's-wort
DESCRIPTION Leafy herb with bright yellow flowers in branching terminal clusters
HABITAT Fields; roadsides; waste places
HEIGHT 12–30 ins (30–75 cm)
FLOWER Cluster, with each flower ¾–1 in (2–2.5 cm) in diameter
FLOWERING June–September
LEAVES Small, elliptical, 1–2 ins (2.5–5 cm) long, opposite

GORDON'S BLADDERPOD
(LESQUERELLA GORDONII)

Gordon's Bladderpod is an annual wildflower that grows in sandy or gravelly ground in desert areas. It is a low-growing plant, with several long, trailing stems, which turn up at the ends, bearing long, lanceolate, strap-like leaves. The leaves nearest the base of the plant are sometimes slightly toothed. The bright yellow flowers are borne in loose raceme clusters at the ends of the stems and have four rounded petals. Fendler's Bladderpod (*L. fendleri*) is found in the same general area, and has very similar yellow flowers, but it is a tufted, more tightly packed, gray-green perennial without trailing stems. It also prefers rocky or sandy soil, and as it flowers so early in the season it makes a splash of bright color against the drab ground in early spring.

FAMILY Mustard
DESCRIPTION Open silver-gray plant with slender trailing stems turning up at the tips, and yellow flowers in loose racemes
HABITAT Sandy or gravel deserts
HEIGHT Trailing, 6 ins (15 cm)
FLOWER Radially symmetrical, ½ in (1.25 cm) in diameter
FLOWERING April–June
LEAVES Lanceolate, 4 ins (10 cm) long

FRINGED PUCCOON; FRINGED GROMWELL (LITHOSPERMUM INCISUM)

FAMILY Borage
DESCRIPTION A hairy plant with a clump of leafy stems and fringed, yellow, trumpet-shaped flowers springing from upper leaf axils
HABITAT Open plains; dry foothills
HEIGHT 3–20 ins (8–50 cm)
FLOWER Radially symmetrical, ½–1½ ins (1.25–3.75 cm) in diameter
FLOWERING May–June
LEAVES Narrowly lanceolate, ¾–2 ins (2–5 cm) long

Fringed Puccoon is a small, leafy plant, with several thick stems clustered together on each plant. The showy yellow flowers are borne on stems springing from the leaf axils, and are trumpet-shaped with a long, narrow tube that flares out suddenly into five rounded lobes that are irregularly toothed. There are 18 species in this genus found across North America, some of which have white flowers. The hard nut-like seeds are not produced from the showy flowers but from smaller ones that appear later in the season. The plant has been used medicinally for thyroid problems, or as a contraceptive.

BIRD'S-FOOT TREFOIL
(LOTUS CORNICULATUS)

Bird's-foot Trefoil is another plant that has been introduced from Europe, and is now found across much of North America except western Canada and the Arctic. Although it is quite easy to find in most areas, it does tend to be a bit rarer in the southern states. The shape of the seed pods gives this plant its common name – they fan out and resemble a bird's claw. Bird's-foot Trefoil is a creeper, with trailing stems which often root where they touch the ground. It has pinnate leaves, and a rather loose umbel clusters of yellow, pea-like flowers. The flowers become tinged with red as they mature and wither away.

FAMILY Pea

DESCRIPTION Trailing stems with turned up tips, stalks with loose clusters of yellow pea-like flowers springing for leaf axils. Stems often root where they touch the ground

HABITAT Meadows; lawns; very damp ground

HEIGHT Creeper, 2–4 ins (5–10 cm)

FLOWER Loose umbel cluster, each flower ¼–½ in (0.5–1.25 cm) in diameter

FLOWERING May–September

LEAVES Pinnate, three at tip, two at junction of stem, ¼–¾ in (0.5–1.8 cm) long

YELLOW SKUNK CABBAGE
(LYSICHITON AMERICANUS)

Skunk Cabbage gets its common name from the very fetid smell of the sap and flowers, which resembles the odor of a skunk and is designed to attract flies to pollinate the flowers. The tiny flowers are densely clustered in a long spike that is partly enclosed in the large and distinctive cream or yellow-colored bract. The bright green oval leaves spring from the base of the plant and can grow up to 5 feet (150 cm) in length, standing erect in a cluster. This is the only species of this genus found in North America, although other species are numerous further south in the tropics. American Indians once dug up and baked the rather fleshy underground stem of Yellow Skunk Cabbage to supplement their winter diet, and it is still often dug up and eaten by wild animals today.

FAMILY Arum
DESCRIPTION Cluster of giant leaves around a stout stalk bearing a spike of tiny flowers with a large yellow or yellow-cream bract, open on one side
HABITAT Swamps
HEIGHT 12–22 ins (30–55 cm)
FLOWER Spike, 8 ins (20 cm) long
FLOWERING March–July
LEAVES Oval, upright, 1–5 ft (30-150 cm) long

FRINGED LOOSESTRIFE
(LYSIMACHIA CILIATA)

FAMILY Primrose

DESCRIPTION Erect stem, sometimes branching, bearing yellow flowers on slender arched stems springing from leaf axils

HABITAT Shallow ponds; stream edges

HEIGHT 4–48 ins (10–120 cm)

FLOWER Radially symmetrical, ¾ in (2 cm) in diameter

FLOWERING June–August

LEAVES Ovate, opposite, 1–2 ins (2.5–5 cm) long, and fringed with stiff hairs

The long, lanceolate to ovate leaves of Fringed Loosestrife are fringed with stiff hairs – hence the plant's common name. They are arranged in opposite pairs along the erect stem, which is sometimes branched, and sometimes single. The solitary yellow flowers have five broad petals with tiny teeth at the tip and a sharp central point. They are borne at the end of short stalks that spring from the leaf axils and usually point outwards, although they can also be seen hanging down. There are 16 species in this genus found across North America, some native and some naturalized from Europe.

SWAMP CANDLES;
(LYSIMACHIA TERRESTRIS) YELLOW LOOSESTRIFE

Swamp Candles is a native of eastern North America, but was introduced to the cranberry bogs of western Washington by accident and has become established there, spreading quickly via underground stems. It is a slender plant, with an erect, leafy stem, and a raceme spike of attractive yellow flowers that can be very showy. Each flower has a circle of dark red spots on the inner end of the pointed petals. Its lanceolate leaves are arranged in opposite pairs along the stem and can be 5 feet (150 cm) long. There are 16 species of this genus, spread across the whole of North America. Swamp Candles prefers to grow in damp and boggy places.

FAMILY Primrose
DESCRIPTION Erect, leafy plant topped with a raceme spike of yellow flowers
HABITAT Swamps and bogs
HEIGHT 8–48 ins (20–120 cm)
FLOWER Raceme spike, each flower ½–¾ in (1.25–2 cm) long
FLOWERING June–August
LEAVES Narrowly lanceolate, 1½–4 ins (4–10 cm) long, arranged opposite

TUFTED LOOSESTRIFE
(LYSIMACHIA THYRSIFLORA)

FAMILY Primrose
DESCRIPTION Erect stemmed plant, with
evenly-spaced leaves and yellow
flowers in a rounded raceme cluster
borne on a slender stem springing
from the leaf axil
HABITAT Swamps; ditches; lakes
HEIGHT 8–32 ins (20–80 cm)
FLOWER Rounded raceme cluster, each
flower ¼ in (0.5 cm) long
FLOWERING May–June
LEAVES Lanceolate, opposite, up to
6 ins (15 cm) long

Tufted Loosestrife prefers to grow in very
wet swamps, flooded ditches, and around
lakes. It is found across much of North
America except the far south. It has an erect
stem with long, lanceolate leaves arranged at
equal intervals in opposite pairs. The bright
yellow flowers have erect stamens, giving
them a fuzzy appearance, and are borne in
dense raceme clusters set around the middle
of the stem, which spring from the leaf axils.
Tufted Loosestrife will easily hybridize with
Swamp Candles (*L. terrestris* – see page 71),
creating plants with flower clusters both in
the middle and in elongated clusters at the
top of the stem.

WHORLED LOOSESTRIFE
(LYSIMACHIA QUADRIFOLIA)

The whorled leaves of Whorled Loosestrife are quite distinctive, as are the dark-streaked petals. It has a tall, erect stem with light green, long, and lanceolate leaves arranged in groups of three to six at regular intervals. The small and star-like yellow flowers are marked with red dots and often streaked right up to the tip. They have five petals and are held at the tips of slender stalks that spring from the leaf axils. Early colonists are reported to have used Whorled Loosestrife to soothe and calm their oxen, and American Indians made a medicinal tea from the plant, which they used to treat kidney and bowel problems.

FAMILY Primrose

DESCRIPTION Erect plant with whorled leaves, yellow star-like flowers on stalks rising from leaf axils

HABITAT Open woodland; fields

HEIGHT 12–34 ins (30–85 cm)

FLOWER Radially symmetrical, ½ in (1.25 cm) in diameter

FLOWERING May–August

LEAVES Lanceolate, in whorls of 4 or more, each 2–4 ins (5–10 cm) long

NORTHERN BLAZINGSTAR
(MENTZELIA LAEVICAULIS
(NUTTALLIA LAEVICAULIS))

Northern Blazingstar is a medium-height plant, with a stout white stem that branches towards the top. Each branch bears a star-like lemon yellow flower with lanceolate, pointed petals. Despite its preference for a rather arid habitat, the flowers are very showy and attractive. The leaves are long, narrow and lanceolate, with large and irregular teeth and barbed hairs that stick to clothing. Other species of *Mentzelia* have Stickleaf as part of their common name because of these barbed hairs. Eveningstar (*M. decapetala*) looks very similar to Northern Blazingstar, but has creamy-white flowers. Despite the similarity in common names, Northern Blazingstar is not related to the *Liatris* genus of blazing stars, which belong to the Aster family.

FAMILY Stickleaf
DESCRIPTION Stout, branching plant, with many star-like, feathery yellow flowers
HABITAT Dry, gravelly, or sandy soil
HEIGHT 12–32 ins (30–80 cm)
FLOWER Radially symmetrical, 2–5 ins (5–12 cm) in diameter
FLOWERING July–September
LEAVES Narrow, lanceolate, irregularly toothed, 4–12 ins (10–30 cm) in length

COMMON MONKEYFLOWER
(MIMULUS GUTTATUS)

FAMILY Figwort
DESCRIPTION Variable plant, sometimes bushy and sometimes small and spindly, yellow flowers on slender stalks springing from leaf axils
HABITAT Wet ground
HEIGHT 40 ins (100 cm)
FLOWER Irregular with two symmetrical halves, each flower ½–1 in (1.25–2.5 cm) long
FLOWERING July–August
LEAVES Ovate, toothed, clasping, ½–4 ins (1.25–10 cm) long

Common Monkeyflower is hard to identify as plants are very variable. It may be tall and spindly or short and bushy; the smooth stem may be erect or trailing. Its flowers can be solitary or are sometimes borne in a short raceme. The leaves are long and ovate, or rounded, toothed, and clasping. To make matters more confusing there are two other species in parts of the same range also known as Yellow Monkeyflower: *M. moschatus*, a hairy-stemmed plant with an open-throated yellow flower, and *M. glabratus*, which is smooth-stemmed, with an open-throated flower. Over half the 85 species of monkeyflower in North America are found only in California.

YELLOW LOTUS;
(NELUMBO LUTEA) AMERICAN LOTUS

Although its flowers are distinctive, Yellow Lotus can also be easily by recognized by its round floating leaves, which are attached to the leafstalk in the center with veins radiating outwards. It also has leaves held above the water, which stay in a bowl shape. The bright yellow, fragrant flowers have many pointed petals and petal-like sepals. In the center of the flower is a large, rather strange upside-down cone with many small holes, each of which holds a pistil. This develops into the seed receptacle, which is held clear of the water. The young leaves and stalks can be used as a pot herb, while tubers can be cooked and eaten like sweet potatoes.

FAMILY Lotus

DESCRIPTION Aquatic plant with floating round leaves or long-stalked bowl-shaped leaves, and fragrant yellow flowers held on long stalks above the water surface

HABITAT Ponds; slow-flowing streams

HEIGHT 6–36 ins (15–90 cm) above water level

FLOWER Radially symmetrical, 6–10 ins (15–25 cm) in diameter

FLOWERING July–September

LEAVES Floating, round and flat, 12–24 ins (30–60 cm) in diameter; erect, bowl-shaped

YELLOW POND-LILY; INDIAN POND LILY; SPATTERDOCK

(NUPHAR LUTEA)

An aquatic plant, Yellow Pond-lily has heart-shaped leaves with rounded ends, which are borne on very long stalks from stems under the mud so they float on the surface of water. The bright yellow flowers are bowl-shaped, with up to nine petal-like sepals and small, narrow inconspicuous petals hidden away among the stamens. American Indians made a tea from the roots of Yellow Pond Lily to treat blood diseases, heart trouble, and chills with fever, and a poultice for swellings, boils, and wounds. The rhizome was also a traditional folk remedy for impotence, but large doses are potentially toxic. In the northeast there is another Yellow Pond-lily (*N. Variegata*), which also has heart-shaped leaves but has smaller flowers. It is the most common yellow pond-lily in the northeast and is also known as the Bullhead Lily.

FAMILY Water-lily
DESCRIPTION Aquatic plant with floating heart-shaped leaves and bowl-shaped yellow flowers that are sometimes floating and sometimes held above the water surface
HABITAT Ponds; slow-flowing streams
HEIGHT 1–6 ins (2.5–15 cm) above water level
FLOWER Radially symmetrical, 2–4 ins (5–10 cm) in diameter
FLOWERING May–September
LEAVES Floating, cordate, 4–18 ins (10–45 cm) long

COMMON EVENING-PRIMROSE
(OENOTHERA BIENNIS)

FAMILY Evening-primrose
DESCRIPTION Leafy-stalked plant, with large, yellow, lemon-scented flowers
HABITAT Fields; roadsides
HEIGHT 24–60 ins (60–150 cm)
FLOWER Umber cluster, each flower 1–2 ins (2.5–5 cm) in diameter
FLOWERING June–September
LEAVES Lanceolate, toothed, 4–8 ins (10–20 cm) long

Common Evening primrose is a night-blooming biennial – its flowers open in the evening and normally close again by midday. The large, yellow flowers are lemon-scented and are borne at the top of the leafy stalk, which is often hairy and sometimes tinged with purple. Evening primrose oil is a natural source of gamma-linoleic acid, which can help imbalances and abnormalities of essential fatty acids, as well as being useful to treat a wide range of illnesses, including migraine, arthritis, dyslexia, and eczema. The seeds are an important source of food for birds, and American Indians used the root to make a medicinal tea.

COMMON PURSLANE; PUSLEY
(PORTULACA OLERACEA)

Common Purslane is a sprawling creeper only a few inches high, but it may have stems that are over 12 ins (30 cm) long. Although it originates from Europe it has now spread everywhere across North America and is fully naturalized. It has thick, fleshy, smooth, red-purple stems and fleshy, flat, green leaves, which are broadly obovate with a rounded tip, and are sometimes alternate, sometimes opposite. The tiny yellow flowers are usually solitary but sometimes form small clusters. Common Purslane is high in iron and its leaves can be used in salads or dried and used as an herb in cooking. American Indians used a poultice made from the plant for burns.

FAMILY Purslane

DESCRIPTION Succulent, fleshy, low-growing plant, thickly-leaved, small yellow flowers in axils of leaves or at stem ends

HABITAT Fields; waste ground

HEIGHT Creeper, 2 ins (5 cm)

FLOWER Radially symmetrical, ¼ in (0.5 cm) in diameter

FLOWERING May–November

LEAVES Obovate with rounded tip, ½–1½ ins (1.5–4 cm) long

STICKY CINQUEFOIL
(POTENTILLA GLANDULOSA)

The name Cinquefoil comes from the French word for five, since many species in this genus have five leaflets. Sticky Cinquefoil is a very pretty wildflower, with several leafy, often reddish stems covered in fine, sticky hairs. Each stem is tipped with a loose cluster of yellow flowers, which have five sepals, five petals and five bracts. The leaves are bipinnate, with ovate, toothed leaflets. There are over 120 species of Cinquefoil found across the whole of North America, many of which are very similar in general appearance, although some species have either white, red, or purple flowers instead of yellow. The species often hybridize, which produces plants with the characteristics of both species, which can make exact identification very difficult. Many of the common species are creepers, but Sticky Cinquefoil can grow up to 22 ins (55 cm) in height. It prefers dry soil, in open areas such as fields.

FAMILY Rose
DESCRIPTION Leafy, many-stemmed plant covered with sticky hairs, yellow flowers in branching clusters
HABITAT Dry, open fields
HEIGHT 22 ins (55 cm)
FLOWER Radially symmetrical, ½–¾ ins (1.25–2 cm) in diameter
FLOWERING May–July
LEAVES Compound pinnate, with ovate sharply-toothed leaflets each ½–2 ins (1.25–5 cm) long

COMMON CINQUEFOIL; OLD-FIELD CINQUEFOIL
(POTENTILLA SIMPLEX)

FAMILY Rose

DESCRIPTION A low, spreading plant, with palmately compound leaves and solitary yellow flowers on a long stem springing from the leaf axil

HABITAT Dry, poor soil

HEIGHT 2–6 ins (5–15 cm)

FLOWER Radially symmetrical, ½–¾ in (1.25–2 cm) in diameter

FLOWERING March–June

LEAVES Palmately compound, five long leaflets 2½ ins (6.5 cm) long

Common Cinquefoil is very similar to Indian Strawberry (*Duchesnea indica*), which has three-lobed leaves, and to Canadian Dwarf Cinquefoil (*P. canadensis*), which has smaller five-lobed leaflets and its first flower rising from the axil of the first leaf. In Common Cinquefoil the solitary flowers are borne at the end of long stalks that rise from the leaf axils, with the first flower springing from the axil of the second leaf. The flowers are bright yellow, with five sepals and five rounded petals. This is a low, spreading plant with supple downy stems and palmately-compound leaves. The leaves have five long, pointed leaflets that are toothed at the tip.

COMMON BUTTERCUP
(RANUNCULUS ACRIS)

Native to Europe, the Common Buttercup was introduced to North America and is now one of the most widespread buttercups across the continent. It is also one of the tallest, with hairy, branching stems and long-stalked, alternate leaves, which are deeply palmately incised into lanceolate, toothed segments. The flowers are typical shiny buttercup yellow — the waxy look is created by a special layer of cells. This species is rather poisonous to animals, but its unpleasant-tasting sap discourages them from grazing on the plant. American Indians made a poultice from the roots for boils and abscesses, using the irritant effect of the sap to burn them off.

FAMILY Buttercup

DESCRIPTION Erect, branching plant, hairy-stemmed, with shiny, bright yellow flowers

HABITAT Damp areas of meadows; damp, disturbed soil

HEIGHT 20–36 ins (50–90 cm)

FLOWER Radially symmetrical, 1 in (2.5 cm) in diameter

FLOWERING May–September

LEAVES Deeply palmately cut into lanceolate, toothed segments, each leaf 1–4 ins (2.5–10 cm) wide

BLACK-EYED SUSAN
(RUDBECKIA HIRTA)

Both a native North American wildflower and a popular garden biennial, Black-eyed Susan has a coarse, erect, rough stem. The long, oblong to lanceolate, leaves have prominent veins, bristly hairs and usually a few sparse teeth on each edge. Lower leaves are borne on short stalks, but the upper ones are often sessile. The attractive flower heads are daisy-like, with 8–21 bright yellow ray florets around a dark purple-brown, dome-shaped central disk. American Indians made a medicinal tea from the roots to treat worms and colds, and as a wash for sores and snakebites. Juice from the root was used to treat earache. Modern science has shown that the plant has immuno-stimulant properties. Black-eyed Susan, which is also sometimes called Yellow Daisy, is the state flower of Maryland. It is very similar in appearance to Cutleaf Coneflower (*R. Laciniata* – see page 88), which has drooping rays and a greeny-brown central disk.

FAMILY Aster
DESCRIPTION Rough-stemmed plant, daisy-like flowers with many yellow rays and a cone-shape brown central disk
HABITAT Prairies; fields; open woodland; waste ground
HEIGHT 14–36 ins (35–90 cm)
FLOWER Compound flower head, 2–3 ins (5–8 cm) in diameter
FLOWERING July–October
LEAVES Oblong to lanceolate, toothed, hairy, 2–7 ins (5–7.5 cm) long

CUTLEAF CONEFLOWER
(RUDBECKIA LACINIATA (RUDBECKIA AMPLA))

FAMILY Aster

DESCRIPTION Tall, erect, and leafy plant, large compound flower heads with drooping yellow rays and a greeny-brown cone-shaped central disk

HABITAT Mountain meadows; damp slopes

HEIGHT 26–120 ins (65–300 cm)

FLOWER Compound flower head, 3–6 ins (8–15 cm) in diameter

FLOWERING June–October

LEAVES Deeply pinnately divided, toothed lobes, 3–8 ins (7.5–20 cm) long; lower on long stalks

A tall, erect plant, Cutleaf Coneflower has a leafy, branching stem with leaves that are long, and deeply pinnately divided into five to seven toothed lobes. The lower leaves have long stalks, while the upper ones are sessile. The stem branches terminate in a solitary large flower head, with six to ten drooping yellow ray florets around a greeny-brown, domed, or conical central disk. American Indians made a medicinal tea with the roots, mixed with others, to relieve indigestion, and the flowers were included in a poultice for burns. Cutleaf Coneflower is similar to Black-eyed Susan (*R. hirta* – see pages 86–7). It is mildly toxic to livestock.

SPOTTED SAXIFRAGE
(SAXIFRAGA BRONCHIALIS (CILIARIA AUSTROMONTANA))

Spotted Saxifrage is a mat-forming plant that spreads to create small clumps of green on rocky ground at higher altitudes. The basal leaves are small, long, and narrow, with stiff hairs along the edges. The many slender stems usually have a few, even smaller, leaves arranged at widely-spaced alternate intervals along their length. The stems terminate in a loose, open, branching cluster of small yellow or creamy-white flowers, spotted inside with purple or dark red. The flowers have five pointed petals, and ten long, and rather spiky stamens. This is a common plant along trails across the mountains, where it prefers apparently inhospitable rocky slopes.

FAMILY Saxifrage
DESCRIPTION Mat-forming plant, with small yellow-white flowers on tall, open, branching stems
HABITAT High altitude rocky slopes
HEIGHT 4–8 ins (10–20 cm)
FLOWER Loose, rounded cluster, each flower ¾ in (2 cm) in diameter
FLOWERING June–August
LEAVES Basal, narrow, and hairy

COMPASS PLANT
(SILPHIUM LACINIATUM)

FAMILY Aster

DESCRIPTION Tall plant with large, rough alternate leaves, yellow flower heads with long rays, a dark yellow central disk and hairy-edged green bracts

HABITAT Prairies

HEIGHT 2–12 ft (60–400 cm)

FLOWER Compound flower head, 3 ins (8 cm) in diameter

FLOWERING June–September

LEAVES Large, deeply pinnately divided, roughly toothed, 12–18 ins (30–45 cm) long

The common name of this plant comes from the leaves, which tend to be aligned north-south. It is very tall with stout, bristly stems bearing very large, rough, dark green leaves, arranged alternately. The leaves are deeply pinnately divided, with the segments irregularly and sharply toothed along the edges. The flower heads are daisy-like, with bright yellow ray florets around a darker yellow central disk. American Indians made a medicinal tea from the roots, and a root tea was also used traditionally for coughs, lung problems and asthma. The stems of Compass Plant exude a resinous sap that can be chewed like gum after it hardens.

BLUE-STEMMED GOLDENROD;
(SOLIDAGO CAESIA) WREATH GOLDENROD

The slender, smooth, arching stem of Blue-stemmed Goldenrod is more purple than blue, often with a whitish, waxy bloom. It bears alternate, elliptical, sessile and toothed leaves with sharply pointed tips. The yellow flowers are borne in scattered, rounded clusters from the leaf axils, with a larger terminal cluster. Individual florets are tiny and have only three to four rays. There are around 90 species in this genus across North America, all with yellow or yellow-cream colored flowers. Wand Goldenrod (*S. stricta*) also has scattered flower clusters, but is found south from New Jersey and has narrow, scale-like leaves.

FAMILY Aster
DESCRIPTION Smooth-stemmed, arching plant with scattered clusters of yellow flowers in leaf axils
HABITAT Woods; clearings
HEIGHT 8–40 ins (20–100 cm)
FLOWER Rounded clusters, each flower ¼ in (0.5 cm) long
FLOWERING August–October
LEAVES Elliptical, sessile, toothed, 2½–5 ins (6.5–12.5 cm) long

CANADA GOLDENROD; MEADOW GOLDENROD

(SOLIDAGO CANADENSIS)

Canada Goldenrod is one of the most common goldenrods to be found in North America, although it is slightly less common in the western states. A showy perennial, it has a stout, hairy stem with long, lanceolate, finely-hairy leaves, which have three prominent veins. The leaves are arranged alternately along the stem and are dark green in color. The tiny yellow flowers form a long, flat-topped cluster along the arching branches, creating a large, handsome panicle in late summer. American Indians used the crushed root to soothe burns, and made a tea from the flowers to use for snakebite and fever. Goldenrods are often blamed for triggering hayfever, but generally it is the less obvious ragweed flowers that are the true culprit.

FAMILY Aster

DESCRIPTION Tall, leafy, hairy-stemmed plant with arching stems ending in a panicle of tiny yellow flowers

HABITAT Meadows; open woodland

HEIGHT 1–5 ft (30–150 cm)

FLOWER Large panicle of tiny flower heads, each ⅛ in (0.3 cm) long

FLOWERING July–September

LEAVES Lanceolate, hairy, 2–5 ins (5–12.5 cm) long

SWEET GOLDENROD
(SOLIDAGO ODORA)

FAMILY Lily

DESCRIPTION Tall, smooth-stemmed plant, with clustered panicles of tiny yellow flowers on arching branches

HABITAT Dry meadows; open woods

HEIGHT 12–48 ins (30–120 cm)

FLOWER Large panicle, each flower ⅛ in (0.3 cm) in length

FLOWERING July–October

LEAVES Narrow, lanceolate, smooth and with small translucent dots, 1–4 ins (2.5–10 cm) long

Sweet Goldenrod has a smooth stem, with long, narrow, lanceolate, smooth, and alternate leaves, which on close inspection have tiny translucent spots. It is instantly identifiable by the scent of anise that its leaves give off when they are crushed. The small flower heads are arranged along only one side of slightly arching branches, making a large, and rather open yellow panicle. A tea can be made from the leaves or from the dried flowers, and this was once used for colic, stomach cramps, colds, dysentery, and measles, and as a wash to cure rheumatism, headaches, and neuralgia.

ROUGH-STEMMED GOLDENROD
(SOLIDAGO RUGOSA)

Rough-stemmed Goldenrod has a long stem, with small, yellow flowers clustered along arching branches to form a roughly triangular-shaped showy panicle. It can be distinguished from other goldenrods by its rough, very hairy stem, and its leaves, which are long, sharply toothed, hairy, rough, and wrinkled – the lower leaves can be as long as 12 inches (30 cm). The leaves are alternate and are often deeply veined. Rough-stemmed Goldenrod can create a mass of color in once-cultivated fields, but also grows along roads and at woodland edges. There are around 90 species of Goldenrod across the whole of North America.

FAMILY Aster
DESCRIPTION Tall, hairy-stemmed plant with small yellow flowers clustered in branching panicles
HABITAT Roadsides; woodland edges; neglected fields
HEIGHT 1–6 ft (30–180 cm)
FLOWER Panicle cluster, each flower $\frac{1}{8}$ in (0.3 cm) long
FLOWERING July–November
LEAVES Rough, sharply-toothed, hairy and wrinkled, 1$\frac{1}{2}$–5 ins (4–12.5 cm) long

COMMON DANDELION
(TARAXACUM OFFICINALE)

FAMILY Aster

DESCRIPTION Basal rosette of toothed and lobed leaves, with a central stalk bearing one flower head made up of numerous yellow rays

HABITAT Waste ground; roadsides; fields; garden lawns

HEIGHT 3–8 ins (8–20 cm)

FLOWER Compound flower head, 1–2 ins (2.5–5 cm) in diameter

FLOWERING March–September

LEAVES Basal rosette, deeply toothed and lobed, 2–16 ins (5–40 cm) long

Originally from Eurasia, the Common Dandelion is now found across most of the world – particularly in suburban lawns. The bright green leaves are deeply and irregularly toothed and lobed. The flower stem rises from the center of the basal rosette and exudes a milky sap when broken. The flower head is made up of many bright yellow rays. A tea made from the roots of Common Dandelion is used to treat liver, gallbladder, kidney, and bladder problems; it has been scientifically proven that there are anti-inflammatory compounds in both the root and the leaves. The young leaves can be cooked and eaten as greens.

YELLOW GOATSBEARD
(TRAGOPOGON DUBIUS)

A native wildflower from Europe, Yellow Goatsbeard has established itself across most of North America. The flower looks rather like that of a dandelion, but the leaves are long and grass-like. It is a biennial, with a coarse stem, long, pointed, clasping leaves, and one yellow flower head, which opens early in the day but is usually closed by midday. The seeds each have feather-like bristles, and as they ripen form a large, downy sphere, very like that of a dandelion but much larger. The leaves can be eaten in salads or cooked as greens, and the tap root cooked like a potato, or roasted and ground to make a coffee substitute.

FAMILY Aster

DESCRIPTION Smooth-stemmed plant with long, grass-like leaves and a single compound flower with many yellow rays

HABITAT Fields; roadsides; waste places

HEIGHT 1–3 ft (30–90 cm)

FLOWER Compound flower head, 1½–2 ins (3.75–5 cm) in diameter

FLOWERING July–August

LEAVES Basal and clasping, broad narrowing to a pointed tip, 12 ins (30 cm) long

STREAM VIOLET; PIONEER VIOLET; SMOOTH YELLOW VIOLET
(VIOLA GLABELLA)

The Stream Violet is very common and is often found in the damp, shaded places across its range. It is a quite low-growing plant, although its heart-shaped leaves with their finely-toothed edges are borne on long, slender stalks. The small, bright yellow flower is the typical violet shape, and the lower three petals have very fine maroon lines radiating out from the base. As in most other western violets, the lower central petal also acts as a landing place for insects coming to find the nectar and pollinate the flower. There are around 80 species of wild violet across North America and many more are cultivated for their attractive flowers, although most of these are descendants of wild European species. The flowers can vary in color from deep purple and blue to yellow and white.

FAMILY Violet

DESCRIPTION Low-growing plant with heart-shaped leaves on leaning or erect stems and irregular yellow flowers on slim stalks

HABITAT Damp woodland; stream edges

HEIGHT 3–12 ins (8–30 cm)

FLOWER Irregular with two symmetrical halves, $\frac{1}{2}$–$\frac{3}{4}$ in (1.25–2 cm) in diameter

FLOWERING March–June

LEAVES Cordate, finely-toothed, $1\frac{1}{4}$–$3\frac{1}{2}$ ins (3–9 cm) in length on long stalks

REDWOOD VIOLET;
EVERGREEN VIOLET (VIOLA SEMPERVIRENS)

FAMILY Violet

DESCRIPTION Creeping plant forming mats of thick leathery leaves, bright yellow flowers on short stalks

HABITAT Damp woodland

HEIGHT Creeper, 5 ins (12 cm)

FLOWER Irregular with two symmetrical halves, ½ in (1.25 cm) in diameter

FLOWERING April–June

LEAVES Cordate, thick and leathery, finely-toothed and scalloped, ½–1 in (1.25–2.5 cm) in width

Redwood Violet is a creeper with broad, thick, leathery, heart-shaped leaves that form a dense mat on the ground. Although it is low-growing it can produce stems up to 12 ins (30 cm) in length. The leaves are finely toothed and scalloped and have quite long stalks. The flowers hang from short stalks just above the level of the leaves and are the typical violet shape, with two upper petals and three lower. The petals are yellow, but the lower three are lightly veined with maroon and the central one has a short, backward-pointing spur. This is one of the most common wildflowers in the redwood forests, and is a popular plant in wildflower gardens.

YARROW; SNEEZEWEED; MILFOIL
(ACHILLEA MILLEFOLIUM)

Yarrow is a perennial plant, which not only occurs in North America but also in Eurasia. Its Latin name honors the Greek Achilles, who is supposed to have used a poultice made from the flowers to stop wounds bleeding on the battlefield. Early Americans used Yarrow for the same purpose, although it can cause dermatitis. It is a fibrous-stemmed plant with aromatic, blue-green, feathery leaves, and tiny white flowers in large, rounded, flat-topped, terminal clusters. There is also an unusual form with rose-pink flowers, which is sometimes transplanted into gardens. Yarrow is part of the Aster family, which includes sunflowers and sneezeweeds.

FAMILY Aster

DESCRIPTION Fibrous-stemmed plant with fern-like leaves and a flat-topped cluster of white flowers

HABITAT Open areas; fields; waste ground

HEIGHT 12–39 ins (30–100 cm)

FLOWER Flat-topped corymb cluster, each flower 2–5 ins (5–12.5 cm) in diameter

FLOWERING May–October

LEAVES Lance-shaped, thin, finely-pinnately divided into segments, 1½ ins (4 cm) wide

VANILLA LEAF; DEER FOOT
(ACHLYS TRIPHYLLA)

Vanilla Leaf is a rather unusual-looking plant that apparently has twin stems — one of which is the stalk or petiole of the leaf and the other that of the flower. The leaf is more or less round in shape, but is deeply incised so it is divided into three fan-shaped leaflets, which are bluntly toothed at the ends. The central leaflet has between five and eight teeth. When they are dried the leaves smell of vanilla, hence the common name. The flower head is a dense spike of very small white flowers. There are only two species in this genus found in North America — the other is California Vanilla Leaf (*A. californica*), which is found nearer the coast. It looks very similar, but the central leaflet has more teeth — sometimes as many as twelve. Vanilla Leaf prefers to grow in the shade of woodland, and flowers early in the season, between April and June.

FAMILY Barberry
DESCRIPTION A slender petiole with a round leaf divided into three fan-shaped leaflets, with a matching slender stalk ending in a short spike of white flowers
HABITAT Woodland
HEIGHT 12–22 ins (30–55 cm)
FLOWER Spike, 1–2 ins (2.5–5 cm)
FLOWERING April–June
LEAVES Orbicular, divided into three fan-shaped leaflets, 2–4 ins (5–10 cm) long

WATER PLANTAIN
(ALISMA PLANTAGO-AQUATICA)

FAMILY Water Plantain
DESCRIPTION Aquatic plant with basal leaves, clusters of small white flowers at the ends of whorled branches
HABITAT Shallow water; marshes
HEIGHT 36–50 ins (90–125 cm)
FLOWER Rounded cluster, each flower ¼–½ in (0.5–1.25 cm) in diameter
FLOWERING July–August
LEAVES Ovate, long-stalked, 1–6 ins (2.5–15 cm) long

A spindly plant, Water Plantain has long ovate leaves above water that spring from the base on long stalks. The leaves underwater are much narrower and more linear. The tiny flowers are borne in open, umbel-like clusters of four or more at the ends of the whorled branches. They are usually white, or sometimes pale pink. Each flower has three sepals, three rounded petals, and several stamens and pistils in a ring. American Indians made a poultice from the root to apply to bruises, swellings, and wounds, and in Chinese medicine the plant is used as a diuretic. Scientific experiments show that it may lower blood pressure and reduce glucose levels.

PEARLY EVERLASTING
(ANAPHALIS MARGARITACEA)

Occurring in both North America and Eurasia, Pearly Everlasting is a perennial plant with a thick, white, woolly stem. The long, thin alternate dark green leaves are smooth above and densely hairy beneath and the rounded cluster of spherical pearly-white flowers is borne at the end of the stems. Male and female flowers grow on separate plants; the male flower can easily be distinguished by a yellow tuft in its center. The flowers remain intact after they are dried, so are useful for flower arrangements. American Indians made a medicinal tea from this plant to cure colds, coughs, and throat infections, and a poultice for burns, sores, and bruising.

FAMILY Aster

DESCRIPTION Woolly-stemmed plant, with dark green leaves and a rounded cluster of flower heads with pearly white bracts

HABITAT Dry fields; roadsides; waste ground

HEIGHT 12–36 ins (30–90 cm)

FLOWER Rounded cluster, each flower ¼ in (0.5 cm) in diameter

FLOWERING July–September

LEAVES Narrowly lanceolate, hairy underside, up to 5 ins (12.5 cm) long

YERBA MANSA
(ANEMOPSIS CALIFORNICA)

Yerba Mansa is an attractive perennial plant, having what looks like a very large showy flower with a cone-shaped center and long white petals. In fact this is a flower head – the cone is a cluster of tiny, yellow flowers and the white "petals" are bracts. The flower head is held at the end of a long, hairy stalk, which springs from the center of a cluster of large, gray-green oblong leaves on long stalks. Yerba Mansa needs good soil, damp conditions, and sun to grow well – it does not like shaded places and cannot tolerate coarse soil or drought. There is only one species found in North America, and this grows wild only across the southwest, but others are found in eastern Asia. The root of Yerba Mansa is quite pleasant-smelling, and has been used to treat cuts and burns and as a poultice for rheumatism.

FAMILY Lizard's-tail
DESCRIPTION Gray-green plant with long, erect leaves, and cone-shaped flower spike
HABITAT Damp areas, particular if salty or alkaline
HEIGHT 12–18 ins (30–45 cm)
FLOWER Cone-shaped spikes, each 1–2 ins (2.5–5 cm)
FLOWERING May–August
LEAVES Oblong, erect, up to 6 ins (15 cm) long

INDIAN HEMP (APOCYNUM CANNABINUM)

FAMILY Dogbane

DESCRIPTION Erect, branching plant with reddish stems and pale green leaves, many erect clusters of small greenish-white flowers

HABITAT Roadsides; thicket edges

HEIGHT 12–24 ins (30–60 cm)

FLOWER Cyme cluster, each flower ¼ in (0.5 cm) in diameter

FLOWERING June–August

LEAVES Lanceolate to obovate, sharply-pointed tip, 1–3 ins (2.5–7.5 cm) long

The scientific name *apocynum* means "noxious to dogs" – hence the family name of Dogbane – but most animals tend to avoid the plants in this genus, which are all poisonous. Indian Hemp is an erect and branching plant, with a stem that turns red when the plant is mature and is filled with a milky-white sap. The several branches on the upper stem bear leaves that are pale green above, and usually whitish on the underside. The numerous whitish-green flowers are borne in terminal clusters. American Indians used the berries to make a weak tea for heart problems, and the stem fiber to make cords and cloth.

(ARALIA NUDICAULIS) WILD SARSAPARILLA

The unusual leaves of Wild Sarsaparilla have three separate stalks, each with five to seven ovate and finely toothed leaflets. The leaves are at the end of a long stem, and shade the flowers like an umbrella. The greenish-white flowers are borne at the end of a bare stalk, in globe-shaped umbel clusters. There are usually at least three separate clusters on each stalk – sometimes as many as seven. The rhizomes are aromatic and can be dried and used as a substitute for sarsaparilla. American Indians made it into a pleasant-flavored drink, which was also used as a tonic. A poultice of fresh root was used to relieve sores, burns, and boils, reduce swelling and cure infection.

FAMILY Ginseng

DESCRIPTION Leafy plant, shading small greenish-white flower round clusters on a short stalk

HABITAT Woodland

HEIGHT 9–24 ins (22–60 cm)

FLOWER Globe-shaped umbel clusters, 1½–2 ins (3.75–5 cm) in diameter

FLOWERING May–August

LEAVES Long stalked, 8–20 ins (20–50 cm) in three sections, each divided into 3–5 ovate leaflets, finely-toothed

SEGO LILY
(CALOCHORTUS NUTTALLII)

Although it is rather a small plant, Sego Lily is very attractive when in flower. It has a stout, straight, erect stem, usually without any branches, and with only a few long, narrow leaves along its length, the edges of which are rolled upwards. The bowl-shaped flowers are usually white but are sometimes tinted pink or lavender, and are marked with deep yellow at the base, with a fringe around the paler, circular central gland, and red or purple crescent marks above. The flowers have three very broad, rounded petals and three shorter, pointed sepals and are borne in a loose umbel-like cluster, with a maximum of three flowers on each stem. The Sego Lily is a perennial that grows from a bulb, which is edible – Mormon settlers used it to supplement their diet when other food was scarce. It is Utah's state flower, but is also quite common in other states across western central North America.

FAMILY Lily
DESCRIPTION Cluster of erect stems, with sparse leaves, bearing showy, white, bowl-shape flowers in a cluster
HABITAT Dry soil on plains and sagebrush; coniferous woods
HEIGHT 6–8 ins (15–45 cm)
FLOWER Radially symmetrical, 1–2 ins (2.5–5 cm) in diameter
FLOWERING May–June
LEAVES Linear, narrow, 2–4 ins (2.5–5 cm) long, edges rolled upwards

SHEPHERD'S PURSE (CAPSELLA BURSA-PASTORIS)

FAMILY Mustard
DESCRIPTION A small plant, topped with a
cluster of tiny white flowers, heart-
shaped flat seed pods on short, fine
stalks along the stem
HABITAT Gardens; waste ground; edges
of fields
HEIGHT 6–24 ins (16–60 cm)
FLOWER Elongated cluster, each flower
¼ in (0.5 cm) in diameter
FLOWERING Throughout the year
LEAVES Lanceolate, lobed, 1–2 ins
(2.5–5 cm) long

Shepherd's Purse is native to Europe, but is
now found in most areas of the world. It is a
small plant with a basal rosette of deeply
lobed leaves, and a few smaller, narrower,
arrow-shaped, clasping leaves along the main
stem. The small, elongated cluster of white
flowers is borne at the tip of a long stalk. The
plant gets its common name from the
distinctive, elongated, heart-shaped, and flat
seed pods, which are the same general shape
as a medieval shepherd's purse. The leaves can
be used in salads, although they may be rather
peppery, and the dried seeds as seasoning in
soups and stews. A medicinal tea from the
seeds and leaves is used to stop bleeding.

(CORNUS CANADENSIS) BUNCHBERRY

Bunchberry is a small but quite attractive plant, with a flower head that looks like a large, white flower. It has several erect stems, each with a whorl of six long, ovate, pointed leaves, which have veins that curve in an arc from the central midrib. The flower head is held just above the leaves on a short stalk, and is made up of many tiny, yellowish-green central florets surrounded by four large white petal-like sepals, which together look like one flower. It winter it has scarlet berries, which are edible. Bunchberry is a native American wildflower, but is also found northeast Asia. American Indians made a tea from the leaves for aches, pains, fevers, and as an eyewash.

FAMILY Dogwood
DESCRIPTION Clusters of stems, with a whorl of bright green leaves below a showy flower cluster on a short stalk
HABITAT Cool woodland
HEIGHT 3–8 ins (8–20 cm)
FLOWER Radially symmetrical flower head, 1½ in (3.75 cm) in diameter
FLOWERING May–July
LEAVES Narrowly ovate, pointed, whorled, ¾–3 ins (2–7.5 cm) long

QUEEN ANNE'S LACE; WILD CARROT (DAUCUS CAROTA)

FAMILY Carrot
DESCRIPTION Hairy-stemmed plant with several large, flat-topped, umbel clusters of tiny white flowers
HABITAT Waste ground; dry fields; roadsides
HEIGHT 12–18 ins (30–45 cm)
FLOWER Compound umbel cluster, 4–5 ins (10–12 cm) in diameter
FLOWERING May–October
LEAVES Pinnately divided into narrow segments, 2–6 ins (5–15 cm) long

Originally a native of Europe, Queen Anne's Lace was introduced to North America many years ago and is now widespread except in the Arctic — in some areas it is considered to be an invasive weed. It has a bristly-haired stem and rather feathery green leaves and the attractive white flower clusters often have one single red-purple flower at the center. The ancestor of the carrot, the leaves smell carrot-like when crushed and the root can be cooked and eaten. It is important to be very sure of the exact identification, as this plant may easily be confused with Poison Hemlock (*Conium maculatum*), which has a purple-spotted stem and is extremely poisonous.

SQUIRREL-CORN
(DICENTRA CANADENSIS)

Squirrel-corn gets its common name from the tubers, which are yellow and resemble corn kernels. It is very similar in appearance to Dutchman's Breeches (*D. cucullaria* — see pages 116–7) and occupies the same habitat and range, but its flowers are narrower and more heart-shaped. The compound gray-green leaves spring from the base of the plant on long stalks, and have deeply cleft leaflets, which makes them look quite feathery. The flowers are white in color and are very fragrant. Since they are so long, few insects and bees have a proboscis long enough to reach the nectar so many merely snip a hole in the side of the flower to reach it.

FAMILY Fumitory
DESCRIPTION Feathery, basal leaves, with clusters of heart-shaped white flowers at the end of a leafless stalk
HABITAT Rich woodlands
HEIGHT 5–10 ins (12.5–25 cm)
FLOWER Elongated raceme cluster, each flower ½ in (1.25 cm) in length
FLOWERING April–May
LEAVES Basal, compound, deeply cleft, feathery, 4 ins (10 cm) long

DUTCHMAN'S BREECHES
(DICENTRA CUCULLARIA)

The shape of the flowers, which have two long spurs and look like tiny pairs of pants hanging upside down from the bare stem, gives Dutchman's Breeches its unusual common name. The flowers are white, sometimes tipped with yellow, and as they are very long they have the same pollination problems as Squirrel-corn (*D. canadensis* – see page 115) – it can be quite difficult to find a flower that has not been snipped open at the side by a bee after the nectar. The gray-green leaves spring from the base of the plant on long stalks, and are compound, with deeply-cleft leaflets, which makes them look very feathery. Iroquois Indians used the leaves to make a rub for athletes, while for the Menomini the plant was a powerful love charm that could attract a woman even against her will. However, Dutchman's Breeches is poisonous to grazing cattle and may cause a skin rash in humans.

FAMILY Fumitory
DESCRIPTION Feathery, basal leaves, with a leafless stalk bearing clusters of white pantaloon-shaped flowers
HABITAT Rich woodlands
HEIGHT 5–10 ins (12.5–25 cm)
FLOWER Elongated raceme cluster, each flower ¾ in (2 cm) in length
FLOWERING April–May
LEAVES Basal, compound, deeply cleft, feathery, 3–6 ins (7.5–15 cm) long

EASTERN SHOOTINGSTAR; PRAIRIE POINTERS (DODECATHEON MEADIA)

FAMILY Primrose

DESCRIPTION Basal rosette of dark green leaves with reddish bases, bare flower stalk with umbel cluster of nodding flowers with distinctive backward curving petals

HABITAT Meadows; open woodland; prairies

HEIGHT 9–22 ins (22–55 cm)

FLOWER Umbel cluster, each flower 1 in (2.5 cm) in length

FLOWERING April–July

LEAVES Basal, lanceolate, up to 6 ins (15 cm) in length

Eastern Shootingstar is an attractive medium-size plant, which prefers to grow in open ground in clearings in woodland, or in meadows and fields. It has dark green, basal leaves, which are sometimes tinged with red where they spring from the plant, and a long, smooth, bare stem that ends in a flat-topped umbel cluster of flowers. The petals of each flower point backwards when the flower is fully open, making it look as if it is shooting earthwards. The flowers are usually white, but can sometimes be pink or lilac. There are 15 species in this genus across North America, and as it is an attractive plant it is also often cultivated.

ROUNDLEAF SUNDEW
(DROSERA ROTUNDIFOLIA)

The tiny Roundleaf Sundew is a perennial carnivorous plant – the basal rosette of small, round leaves are reddish due to colored hairs that exude small drops of sticky sap to catch small insects. When an insect lands on the leaf it becomes trapped, and the leaf quickly folds over to digest it. The plant is able to survive in particularly poor soil because it gets most of the nutrients it requires from the bugs it catches. The small flowers are arranged along one side of a leafless stalk in an elongated raceme – they are usually white, but are sometimes pink or red. There are eight species within this genus found across North America.

FAMILY Sundew
DESCRIPTION Carnivorous plant with a basal rosette of small, round, reddisih sticky leaves; white flower in an elongated cluster at the end of a slender stalk
HABITAT Boggy ground
HEIGHT 4–9 ins (10–22 cm)
FLOWER Radially symmetrical, ¼ in (0.5 cm) in diameter
FLOWERING June–August
LEAVES Circular, covered in sticky hairs, ½ in (1.25 cm) across

SPREADING FLEABANE
(ERIGERON DIVERGENS)

FAMILY Aster

DESCRIPTION Branching plant with short hairs, each branch topped with a daisy-like flower head

HABITAT Sandy deserts; plains; open foothills

HEIGHT 6–26 ins (15–65 cm)

FLOWER Compound flower head, 1 in (2.5 cm) in diameter

FLOWERING May–September

LEAVES Lanceolate, tapering to stalk-like base, up to 1 in (2.5 cm) long

Spreading Fleabane is a medium-size plant with a branching stem covered in short hairs and many small, lanceolate leaves arranged alternately. The base leaves are larger and longer, tapering to a stalk-like base, and often arranged in tufts. The flower heads are held at the tips of the branches and usually have lots of very narrow, white, or pinkish ray flowers around a bright yellow, flat central disk – although sometimes the ray florets are entirely missing, leaving only the yellow disk. There are around 140 species of this genus found in North America, most of which are very similar and hard to tell apart.

DESERT TRUMPET;
(ERIOGONUM INFLATUM) INDIANPIPE WEED

With its erect, slender, gray-green stems that are swollen toward the top, the stem branching out just above the inflated section, Desert Trumpet is an odd-looking plant. The bare stems spring from a basal rosette of small, long-stalked, oval to rounded leaves. The tiny white to yellow flowers grow at the tips of slender stalks in small, rounded clusters set in woolly cups — cups around the flowers are a typical feature of species in this genus. A common plant in sandy or rocky desert, the alternative name of Indianpipe Weed comes from American Indians having traditionally used the dried stems as pipes for smoking tobacco.

FAMILY Buckwheat

DESCRIPTION Spindly plant with a basal rosette of oval leaves, tall stems swollen high up just below the branches, tiny yellow flowers in woolly cups at branch ends

HABITAT Sandy or rocky deserts

HEIGHT 9–38 ins (22–95 cm)

FLOWER Rounded cluster, ½ in (1.25 cm) in diameter

FLOWERING March–July

LEAVES Basal rosette, oval, long stalks, 1–2 ins (2.5–5 cm) long

WHITE TROUT LILY
(ERYTHRONIUM ALBIDUM)

The leaves of White Trout Lily are long and elliptical and sheath the base of the stem. The small bell-shaped flower with its curved back petals is borne at the end of a bare stalk, and is white inside but often tinged with lavender outside. There may be several flowers on each plant, each with its own stalk. White Trout Lily has a very similar range and habitat to the Trout Lily (*E. americanum* – see pages 52–3) but its two leaves are distinctly narrower and may not be as mottled. These plants are sometimes known as Dogtooth Violets because of the shape of the underground bulb, although neither are violets. The name Trout Lily refers to the markings on the leaves, which are supposed to resemble those of the Brown Trout.

Traditionally, a poultice of the leaves of White Trout Lily was used to treat ulcers, draw out splinters and reduce swelling. The leaves have been tested scientifically and do soften the skin, but they may also cause an allergic reaction so should not be applied by unqualified practitioners.

FAMILY Lily

DESCRIPTION Sheath of narrow, mottled leaves around the base of a bare stalk bearing a nodding white bell-shaped flower with curved-back petals

HABITAT Woodland; meadows

HEIGHT 4–12 ins (10–30 cm)

FLOWER Radially symmetrical, 1 in (2.5 cm) in diameter

FLOWERING March–May

LEAVES Basal sheath, narrow, elliptical, 2–6 ins (5–15 cm) in length

BONESET (EUPATORIUM PERFOLIATUM)

FAMILY Aster
DESCRIPTION Hairy, branching plant with flat-topped clusters of white flowers
HABITAT Wet meadows; damp woodland
HEIGHT 12–48 ins (30–120 cm)
FLOWER Flat-topped clusters, each flower ¼ in (0.5 cm) long
FLOWERING July–October
LEAVES Lanceolate, toothed, wrinkled, sessile, opposite and perfoliate, 4–8 ins (10–20 cm) long

The name Boneset originated because the leaves were used to treat dengue fever, in which the bones ache as if they were broken. A hairy, branching plant, Boneset has many dense, flat-topped clusters of white to pale purple flowers and long, lanceolate and wrinkled leaves in pairs that are joined at the base so they completely surround the stem. Boneset was used in many home remedies by early settlers, particularly to treat influenza. Recent scientific research suggests that the plant has some immune-system-enhancing properties, but large doses may damage the liver so are very dangerous.

(GLAUX MARITIMA) SEA-MILKWORT

Sea-milkwort is a spreading plant, and often forms quite large patches, but it is not that common in most areas and should not be removed from the wild. It is low-growing and prefers salt water marshes, so it is often found near the shore. Sea-milkwort has a thick, fleshy stem bearing small, oblong to oval, succulent, gray-green leaves arranged in opposite pairs. The small flowers are cup-shaped and usually white, pinky-cream or tinted pale lavender; they have no petals but five petal-like sepals. They are sessile, springing directly from the leaf axils. American Indians once boiled the roots and ate them to induce sleep.

FAMILY Primrose
DESCRIPTION Low-growing plant with small, fleshy oval leaves and tiny white, pink or lavender tinted flowers springing direct from the leaf axils
HABITAT Salt marshes; seashores
HEIGHT 3–12 ins (8–30 cm)
FLOWER Radially symmetrical, ¼ in (0.5 cm) in diameter
FLOWERING July
LEAVES Fleshy, oblong to oval, ½ in (1.25 cm) long

TWINLEAF
(JEFFERSONIA DIPHYLLA)

It is easy to see how the common name of this plant came about – its leaves are in two separate mirror-image halves. They are basal, but borne on the ends of long stalks, and the individual halves are roughly kidney-shaped with rather pointed lobes. The single white flower is attractive, with six to nine petals arranged in a very open bowl shape. Twinleaf is now too rare to harvest on any scale, but Native Americans used its root extensively, making it into a tea that was drunk to treat cramps, spasms, kidney stones, and urinary infections, and applied externally for rheumatism, sores, and ulcers. A very similar-looking plant is Bloodroot (*Sanguinaria canadensis* – see pages 142–3), but it can be distinguished by its different leaves, which are palmately compound. There is only one other twinleaf species, *J. dubia*, which only occurs in Japan.

FAMILY Barberry
DESCRIPTION Low-growing plant with leaves divided lengthwise into two large lobes, white flower at the top of a bare stalk
HABITAT Damp, open woodland
HEIGHT 6–10 ins (15–25 cm)
FLOWER Radially symmetrical, 1 in (2.5 cm) in diameter
FLOWERING April–May
LEAVES Basal, long-stemmed, two symmetrical lobes, 3–6 ins (7.5–15 cm) long

OXEYE DAISY
(LEUCANTHEMUM VULGARE (CHRYSANTHEMUM LEUCANTHEMUM))

FAMILY Aster

DESCRIPTION Multi-stemmed plant with dark green lobed or toothed leaves on long stalks, small upper leaves, and a large, daisy-like flower

HABITAT Fields; meadows; roadsides

HEIGHT 8–32 ins (20–80 cm)

FLOWER Compound flower head, 3 ins (8 cm) in diameter

FLOWERING May–September

LEAVES Lower lanceolate, lobed or deeply toothed, with long petioles, up to 6 ins (15 cm) long; upper smaller, lobed and sessile, 3 ins (7.5 cm) long

Oxeye Daisy is a native of Europe that was introduced to North America, and is now naturalized across much of the continent – although it is more common in the north. A leafy and attractive perennial, it has several stems bearing dark green, lanceolate, lobed, or deeply toothed leaves with long stalks, and smaller, sessile upper leaves. The flowers are borne at the tip of a long, leafless stalk and are daisy-like, with white rays and a bright yellow central disk. Europeans used this plant as a tonic, and American Indians made a tea to treat fever and chapped hands. It does have anti-inflammatory properties, but can cause contact dermatitis, or an allergic reaction.

FALSE LILY-OF-THE-VALLEY
(MAIANTHEMUM DILATATUM)

False Lily-of-the-valley gets its common name from its resemblance to the European plant Lily-of-the-valley (*Convallaria majalis*). False Lily-of-the-valley has heart-shaped leaves, usually two on each stem, and slender racemes of sweet-scented white flowers on long, erect stems. These open into a star-shape with four segments, quite unlike the bell-shaped flowers of true Lily-of-the-valley. False Lily-of-the-valley prefers the shade of woodland, and likes damp soil. It is an attractive perennial that grows from a rhizome, so it is a very useful and pretty ground cover across shaded areas.

FAMILY Lily
DESCRIPTION Low-growing plant, forming small clumps, with heart-shaped leaves and racemes of tiny white flowers on slender stems
HABITAT Damp, shady woods
HEIGHT 6–16 ins (15–40 cm)
FLOWER Elongated raceme cluster, 1–2 ins (2.5–5 cm) in length
FLOWERING May–June
LEAVES Cordate, 2–4 ins (5–10 cm) long

WHITE SWEET CLOVER
(MELILOTUS ALBA)

A native of Eurasia, White Sweet Clover was introduced to North America and is now found across most of the continent, except in the very far north. It can grow extremely tall, and has widely-branched stems bearing three-part, bright green leaves. Each individual leaflet is lanceolate in shape with toothed edges. The flowers are white and pea-like and arranged in long, tapering racemes, on stalks that spring from the leaf axils. The flowers have a strong scent of vanilla or of new-mown hay, particularly when they are crushed, and therefore White Sweet Clover is particularly valued as a source of nectar for honey. There are also two very similar species in North America: Yellow Sweet Clover (*M. officinalis*), which is found in the Rocky Mountains but does not grow as tall, and the quite rare Sour Clover (*M. indica*). Both of these have yellow flowers rather than white.

FAMILY Pea
DESCRIPTION Tall, branching, leafy plant with many racemes of tiny, white, pea-like flowers
HABITAT Fields; roadsides
HEIGHT 2–9 ft (60–270 cm)
FLOWER Raceme, 8 ins (20 cm) long
FLOWERING April–October
LEAVES Compound; three lanceolate, toothed leaflets, each ½–1 in long (1.25–2.5 cm) long

PARTRIDGEBERRY; SQUAW-VINE (MITCHELLA REPENS)

FAMILY Madder
DESCRIPTION Trailing plant with white-veined green leaves and tubular white flowers
HABITAT Woodland
HEIGHT Creeper, 6 ins (15 cm)
FLOWER Radially symmetrical, ½–¾ in (1.25–2 cm) in diameter
FLOWERING May–July
LEAVES Broadly ovate, opposite, shiny green with white veins, up to ¾ in (2 cm) long

Partridgeberry is a trailing creeper and is a useful ornamental ground cover in shady areas, because its shiny evergreen leaves are very attractive with their white veining. The white, tubular flowers are borne in pairs on a single short stem and are very fragrant. The bright red berries are eye-catching and edible, but they have no particular connection with the partridge. The alternative common name of Squaw-vine originates from the historical use of the plant to treat irregular and painful menses, and for pain during childbirth. As a wash it was used for arthritis, rheumatism, and sore nipples. There is only one species of this genus in North America.

FIVESPOT
(NEMOPHILA MACULATA)

Fivespot has many long, slender stalks with pinnately-lobed leaves, arranged in opposite pairs on short stalks. The smooth, bright green leaves usually have between three and nine lobes. Each of the attractive flowers is held at the end of its own long, slender stalk. The flowers are open and bowl-shaped, with five wide lobes that are mainly white, but which have a large, deep purple-blue spot at the tip – hence the common name of Fivespot. This plant is very similar to the well-known western wildflower Baby Blue Eyes (*N. menziesii*), which has pale blue flowers darkening evenly to deep purple at the tip of the lobes.

FAMILY Waterleaf

DESCRIPTION Low-growing plant with slender, branching stems, bearing white, open, bowl-shaped flowers, each petal with a distinctive purple-blue spot at the tip

HABITAT Open hillsides

HEIGHT 3–12 ins (8–30 cm)

FLOWER Radially symmetrical, 1–2 ins (2.5–5 cm) in diameter

FLOWERING April–June

LEAVES Pinnately-lobed, 1–2 ins (2.5–5 cm) long

FRAGRANT WATER-LILY
(NYMPHAEA ODORATA)

True to its name, the Fragrant Water-lily has sweet-smelling white, or occasionally pale yellow, flowers with many pointed petals and numerous bright yellow stamens. The flowers only open in the morning, closing in early afternoon until the following day. The shiny, green, rounded leaves float on the surface of water, and are shiny dark green on the top, and purple-red beneath. Both flowers and leaves are held just above the surface of water at the end of stalks that can be as long as 48 inches (120 cm), which spring from stalks buried in the mud. American Indians made a tea from the spongy roots to treat coughs, tuberculosis, and mouth sores, and a root poultice for swellings. They also ground the seeds for flour, or roasted them like popcorn. Traditionally a root tea was drunk for chronic diarrhea, but large doses may very well be toxic.

FAMILY Water-lily
DESCRIPTION Aquatic plant, with round, floating leaves and white to yellow, many-petalled, floating flower
HABITAT Ponds; slow-flowing streams
HEIGHT 3–5 ins (8–12 cm) above water level
FLOWER Radially symmetrical, 4–5 ins (10–12 cm) in diameter
FLOWERING June–September
LEAVES Floating, orbicular, up to 10 ins (25 cm) in diameter

HOT ROCK PENSTEMON
(PENSTEMON DEUSTUS)

FAMILY Figwort
DESCRIPTION Woody-based plant with clusters of stems, white-pink flowers with leafy bracts, arranged in whorls
HABITAT Open, rocky ground
HEIGHT 9–24 ins (22–60 cm)
FLOWER Tubular, with two symmetrical halves, ½–¾ in (1.25–2 cm) in length
FLOWERING June–July
LEAVES Ovate, sharply toothed, up to 3 ins (7.5 cm) long

Most penstemons have blue-lavender or red flowers, but Hot Rock Penstemon is one of the few species in the genus to have white ones. Its clustered stems spring from a woody base, and bear bright green leaves arranged closely together in opposite pairs. They are long, ovate, and sharply toothed. The white flowers often have fine purplish lines inside, and are tubular, with two symmetrical halves, two lobes pointing upwards and three down. They are arranged in whorls in the axils of leaf-like bracts, creating an elongated, upright cluster. The slightly unpleasant smell that is typical of many penstemons is rather stronger in Hot Rock Penstemon.

ENGLISH PLANTAIN
(PLANTAGO LANCEOLATA)

English Plantain originates from Europe, but has spread widely across much of North America and is fully naturalized. It is often found in garden lawns, along with the Common Dandelion (*Taraxacum officinale* — see page 96). The long, narrow, lance-shaped leaves at the base of the plant have three ribs and parallel veins. The short, cylindrical flower head is held above the leaves at the end of a bare, grooved stalk. Traditionally, a tea made from the leaves was used to cure coughs and bronchial infections, and its effectiveness has been proven scientifically — it contains a mild antibiotic and has an anti-inflammatory action.

FAMILY Plantain
DESCRIPTION Basal rosette of long, narrow leaves, with a central bare flower stalk terminating in a narrow cylindrical spike of white flowers
HABITAT Roadsides; waste ground; garden lawns
HEIGHT 6–22 ins (15–55 cm)
FLOWER Cylindrical head, each flower ¼ in (0.5 cm) long
FLOWERING April–November
LEAVES Narrow, lanceolate, 2–16 ins (5–40 cm) long

MAY-APPLE
(PODOPHYLLUM PELTATUM)

FAMILY Barberry
DESCRIPTION Woodland plant with a
   pretty white flower springing on a
   short stalk from the angle between
   two large, lobed leaves
HABITAT Damp clearings in deciduous
   woodlands
HEIGHT 12–20 ins (30–75 cm)
FLOWER Radially symmetrical, 2 ins
   (5 cm) in diameter
FLOWERING April–June
LEAVES Palmate, deeply lobed, up to
   12 ins (30 cm) wide

May-apple has creeping underground stems
and often forms large, dense patches. It is
quite distinctive, with its pair of large,
deeply-lobed palmate leaves borne on short
stalks at the end of a single stem. The single
apple-blossom-like flower hangs downwards,
and is held at the end of a short stalk that
springs from the angle of the two leaf stalks.
The yellow or red egg-shaped berry is edible,
and can be made into pies and preserves,
although the leaves, roots, and seeds can be
poisonous in large amounts. American Indians
used the roots as a purgative and to treat
hepatitis and fevers and a partly synthetic
derivative is now used in cancer treatments.

WESTERN PASQUEFLOWER; MOUNTAIN PASQUEFLOWER
(PULSATILLA OCCIDENTALIS (ANEMONE OCCIDENTALIS))

Western Pasqueflower grows at high elevations, so it flowers fairly late in the year. It has several softly hairy stems, which spring from basal leaves that are deeply divided into very narrow segments. There are also three smaller, hairy, sessile, and deeply-divided leaves higher up the stems, whorled round just beneath the flowers. The stems terminate in a solitary, bowl-shaped flower with five to seven white or cream petal-like sepals, which are hairy on the back. There are no petals, but a great many stamens, creating the distinctive look of pasqueflowers. The seeds are each tipped with a long plume that creates a feathery, shaggy, rounded seed head.

FAMILY Buttercup

DESCRIPTION Hairy plant with several stems ending in a bowl-shaped, hairy white flower

HABITAT Mountain meadows

HEIGHT 8–22 ins (20–55 cm)

FLOWER Radially symmetrical, 1–2 ins (2.5–5 cm) in diameter

FLOWERING May–September

LEAVES Basal, finely-divided; stem, whorled and narrowly segmented, 1½–3 ins (4–7.5 cm) across

GRASS-LEAF ARROWHEAD
(SAGITTARIA GRAMINEA)

FAMILY Water Plantain
DESCRIPTION Aquatic plant with long, grass-like leaves, bearing white flowers on thin stems with whorled branches
HABITAT Shallow water
HEIGHT 12–24 ins (30–60 cm)
FLOWER Elongated cluster, each flower ½ in (1.25 cm) in diameter
FLOWERING March–November
LEAVES Linear, grass-like, up to 8 ins (20 cm) long

Grass-leaf Arrowhead grows in shallow water and its long, narrow, linear, grass-like leaves spring from the submerged rhizome and stand erect above the water level. The rather spindly flower stalks are also long and rise well above the water. They have small, attractive white flowers, which are whorled on short branches. The flowers have three sepals and three broad white petals and the male and female flowers are borne on the same plant – the upper flowers usually have stamens, while the lower ones have pistils. There are more than 30 species in this genus found in North America.

ARROWHEAD
(SAGITTARIA LATIFOLIA)

An aquatic plant that grows in shallow water, Arrowhead has basal, arrow-shaped leaves, with prominent veining, standing erect above the water level. The small, white flowers are whorled at the ends of long flower stalks, and have three sepals and three broad white petals. Some of the flowers have stamens, while others have many pistils arranged in a sphere. The plant grows from a submerged rhizome, which American Indians made into a medicinal tea that was used to treat indigestion, and into a poultice to apply to wounds and sores. Early settlers cooked and ate the rhizome like a potato, and called the plant Duck Potato.

FAMILY Water Plantain

DESCRIPTION Aquatic plant with arrow-shaped leaves and an elongated spike of small, white flowers

HABITAT Shallow water

HEIGHT 12–36 ins (30–90 cm) above water level

FLOWER Elongated cluster, each flower ½–1½ in (1.25–3.75 cm) in diameter

FLOWERING June–September

LEAVES Basal, arrow-shaped, 4–20 ins (10–50 cm) long

BLOODROOT
(SANGUINARIA CANADENSIS)

Bloodroot is a pretty spring flower, and one of its unusual features is that the flower often appears before the leaf. The flower has many long, narrowly-pointed white petals and a yellow center, and looks rather like that of a water lily. It only opens in full sunlight, closing on dull days and at night. The single basal leaf, which is deeply palmately lobed, curves around the flower stalk. The sap of this plant is bright red-orange – hence its common name – and it was used by American Indians as a dye in craftwork, as war paint and as an insect repellent. They also made a medicinal root tea for lung ailments and rheumatism. It has since been found to inhibit plaque on teeth, and so is sometimes used commercially in toothpastes and mouthwashes. Despite this, the plant is considered to be toxic in quantity and should therefore not be eaten.

FAMILY Poppy
DESCRIPTION Small plant with one palmately-scalloped leaf curling around a flower stalk bearing an open white flower with a yellow feathery center; sap bright red
HABITAT Stream edges; damp woodland
HEIGHT 11 ins (28 cm)
FLOWER Radially symmetrical, 2 ins (5 cm) in diameter
FLOWERING March–June
LEAVES Basal, palmately scalloped into lobes, 4–7 ins (10–17.5 cm) long

BOUNCING BET; SOAPWORT (SAPONARIA OFFICINALIS)

FAMILY Carnation

DESCRIPTION Leafy plant growing in clumps, with dense clusters of sweet-scented pink or white flowers

HABITAT Roadsides; disturbed ground

HEIGHT 12–30 ins (30–75 cm)

FLOWER Rounded cluster, each flower 1 in (2.5 cm) in diameter

FLOWERING July–September

LEAVES Oval, opposite, 1–5 ins (2.5–12.5 cm) long

Originally from Europe, Bouncing Bet was introduced to North America and is now found across the continent. A tall perennial, it has a smooth, thick stem, sometimes with one or two branches, and long, oval leaves arranged in opposite pairs, each leaf with 3–5 conspicuous ribs. The white or very pale pink flowers are in dense, rounded terminal clusters and have notched petals. Bouncing Bet spreads quickly via underground stems and forms quite large colonies. When the foliage is crushed and mixed with water a lather is generated, hence the common name of Soapwort, while Bouncing Bet is an old-fashioned term for a washerwoman.

WHITE CAMPION; EVENING LYCHNIS; WHITE COCKLE
(SILENE LATIFOLIA (LYCHNIS ALBA))

A native wildflower of Europe, White Campion was introduced to North America and is now naturalized across much of the continent. It has a many-branched stem, with long, light green, opposite leaves covered in downy hair. The sweet-scented white flowers open at night, and are pollinated by moths; male and female flowers are on separate plants. It is easy to confuse this plant with Night-flowering Catchfly (*S. noctiflora*), which also has hairy leaves and white flowers, but has sticky hairs and a female flower with three styles, while the female flowers of White Campion have five styles. Occasionally White Campion has pale pink flowers.

FAMILY Carnation
DESCRIPTION Softly-hairy, branching plant, with night-flowering, sweet-scented white flowers
HABITAT Roadsides; waste ground; open fields
HEIGHT 12–36 ins (30–90 cm)
FLOWER Radially symmetrical, 1 in (2.5 cm) in diameter
FLOWERING June–September
LEAVES Lanceolate, opposite, hairy, 1–4 ins (2.5–10 cm) in length

BLADDER CAMPION; MAIDEN'S TEARS
(SILENE VULGARIS (SILENE CUCUBALUS))

Bladder Campion is distinctive because of its inflated, balloon-like calyx, which has clear lengthways veins like other varieties of *Silene*, and also a distinct network of smaller veins. It looks rather like a tiny paper lantern at the base of the flower. The stem of Bladder Campion is not as branched as that of White Campion (*S. latifolia* – see page 145), and the leaves are opposite, smooth, and often clasping. The flower petals are very deeply notched and open at night to be pollinated by moths. Like White Campion, Bladder Campion is a European wildflower that has been introduced to North America and is now naturalized. It can also be confused with Night-flowering Catchfly (*S. noctiflora*), but this species is hairy and sticky, and has much broader leaves. Other similar introductions from Europe include Balkan Catchfly (*S. cserei*), which is almost identical to Bladder Campion, and Forking Catchfly (*S. dichotoma*), which has stalkless flowers.

FAMILY Carnation
DESCRIPTION Night-flowering plant, white flowers with deeply-notched petals and balloon-like inflated calyx, smooth leaves
HABITAT Fields; roadsides
HEIGHT 9–30 ins (22–75 cm)
FLOWER Radially symmetrical, 1 in (2.5 cm) in diameter
FLOWERING April–August
LEAVES Lanceolate, often clasping, opposite, 1–4 ins (2.5–10 cm) long

EARLY MEADOW-RUE
(THALICTRUM DIOICUM)

FAMILY Buttercup

DESCRIPTION Tall, leafy plant with drooping clusters of white flowers on long stalks springing from leaf axils

HABITAT Damp woodland

HEIGHT 8–24 ins (20–60 cm)

FLOWER Rounded clusters, each flower ¼ in (0.5 cm) long

FLOWERING April–May

LEAVES Tripartite, with rounded, lobed leaflets, each up to 2 ins (5 cm) wide

Despite its name, Early Meadow-rue prefers the shaded habitat of damp and rich woodland, although it does flower very early in the year. The roughly-rounded clusters of drooping, greeny-white flowers are held on long stalks and the male and female are on separate plants. Both types have four to five petal-like sepals, but no petals; the male flower has a cluster of long, yellow stamens hanging below the sepals, while the female flower has several long purple pistils instead. The stem has many leaves borne alternately along the stem, each in three parts, with the leaflets rounded and lobed.

RUE ANEMONE; WINDFLOWER
(THALICTRUM THALICTROIDES (ANEMONELLA THALICTROIDES))

Rue Anemone is slender, rather delicate-looking woodland plant, which is often cultivated in wildflower gardens. It has small, ovate stem leaves and either a pair or a whorl of basal leaves divided into three parts, with the leaflets having rounded lobes. The open white flowers, which can be tinged with pink, have 5–11 petal-like sepals, but no true petals, and a feathery cluster of yellow stamens and pistils in the center. American Indians made a tea from the roots to treat diarrhea and vomiting, and early physicians used the root to treat piles, but Rue Anemone is potentially poisonous. It is sometimes classed in the genus *Anemonella*.

FAMILY Buttercup

DESCRIPTION Delicate woodland plant with several open white flowers held above a whorl of three-part leaves

HABITAT Open woodland

HEIGHT 4–8 ins (10–20 cm)

FLOWER Radially symmetrical, 1 in (2.5 cm) in diameter

FLOWERING March–May

LEAVES Basal, whorled, tripartite; leaflets round, lobed, up to 1 in (2.5 cm) long

EASTERN FOAMFLOWER; FALSE MITERWORT

(TIARELLA CORDIFOLIA)

Eastern Foamflower is an attractive woodland wildflower with spiky, feathery, white flowers in an elongated, open cluster. The flowers have five petals and five sepals, with ten fine stamens and one pistil, and their delicate nature makes them look rather like white foam, leading to the Foamflower part of the plant's common name. The leaves spring on long stalks from the base of the plant, and are palmately lobed, deeply indented at the base and sharply toothed – in general shape, they look rather like those of the maple. Eastern Foamflower has underground stems and spreads very quickly to form large colonies, so it is a useful ground cover for a shady woodland garden. American Indians used a tea made from the leaves as a mouthwash and for eye ailments, and a root tea as a diuretic and for diarrhea.

FAMILY Saxifrage
DESCRIPTION Small plant with several basal, palmately-lobed leaves on long stalks, and an elongated cluster of feathery white flowers
HABITAT Woodlands
HEIGHT 6–12 ins (15–30 cm)
FLOWER Elongated cluster, each flower ¼ in (0.5 cm) in diameter
FLOWERING April–May
LEAVES Basal, palmately-lobed, sharp-toothed, hairy, 2–4 ins (5–10 cm) in length

NODDING TRILLIUM
(TRILLIUM CERNUUM)

FAMILY Lily

DESCRIPTION Small plant with a whorl of three large leaves and a nodding white flower on a short, curved stalk

HABITAT Swamps; moist woodland

HEIGHT 5–22 ins (12–55 cm)

FLOWER Radially symmetrical, 1–2 ins (2.5–5 cm) in diameter

FLOWERING May–July

LEAVES Rhomboidal to orbicular, whorled, 2½–4 ins (6.5–10 cm) long

The common name of Nodding Trillium comes partly from the drooping flowers and partly because it has many of its parts in threes. The three, relatively large whorled leaves are almost diamond-shaped and have very short stalks. The flower has three sepals and three petals and nods at the end of a short, downward-curved stalk, so that it hangs beneath the leaves. The flower is white – or sometimes very pale pink – with the petals curved back at the tips, and with pink anthers. There are around 42 species of this genus in North America, but almost all of them are concentrated in the eastern half of the continent.

LARGE-FLOWER TRILLIUM
(TRILLIUM GRANDIFLORUM)

One of the showiest trilliums in North America, Large-flowered Trillium is an attractive plant. The large white flower turns pink as it matures and has three pointed petals and three smaller sepals. It is borne at the end of a short stalk springing from a whorl of three diamond-shaped to ovate, dark green leaves growing at the top of an erect stem. American Indians used the root for many medicinal purposes, and the leaves can be eaten in salads or as greens – but picking them will probably kill the plant. As Large-flowered Trillium is so attractive it is often grown in wildflower gardens, but should never be picked or dug up from the wild.

FAMILY Lily

DESCRIPTION Woodland plant with a whorl of large, diamond-shaped leaves and a large, three-petalled white flower

HABITAT Woodland; thickets

HEIGHT 8–16 ins (20–40 cm)

FLOWER Radially symmetrical, 2–4 ins (5–10 cm) in diameter

FLOWERING April–June

LEAVES Diamond-shaped, pointed, 2–4 ins (5–10 cm) long, short stalk

WESTERN TRILLIUM; WESTERN WAKEROBIN

(TRILLIUM OVATUM)

Western Trillium is found in open woods and is a low-growing plant with white, three-petalled flowers. The petals are quite large and pointed and there are three smaller sepals, and the flower is borne at the end of a short stalk springing from the center of a whorl of three diamond-shaped to ovate, dark green leaves. The leaves are almost sessile and are borne at the top of a bare stem. The alternative common name of Wakerobin comes from the early flowering time of this plant, which is roughly when the robin arrives. There are 42 species in this genus across North America, mostly concentrated in the east of the continent, but with a few in the northwest.

FAMILY Lily
DESCRIPTION Small plant with whorl of large leaves at the top of a bare stem, one white three-petalled flower springing from the center of the whorl on a short stalk
HABITAT Woodland; thickets
HEIGHT 4–6 ins (10–40 cm)
FLOWER Radially symmetrical, 1–3 ins (2.5–8 cm) in diameter
FLOWERING April–June
LEAVES Diamond-shaped, 2–8 ins (5–20 cm) long

SESSILE BELLWORT; WILD OATS
(UVULARIA SESSILIFOLIA)

A common woodland flower within its range, Sessile Bellwort is a rather spindly plant. It has one or more trumpet-shaped, creamy-white or yellowish flowers, which hang down from a short, angled stalk. The sparse leaves are long, oblong, and clasping, and are quite a light green above and whitish beneath. A very similar species, Bellwort (*U. perfoliata*) is distinguished by having perfoliate leaves and orange markings within the trumpet of the flower. There is also a larger version, Large-flowered Bellwort (*U. grandiflora*), which has bright yellow flowers. American Indians used the root of Sessile Bellwort to make a medicinal tea that was used to purify the blood and help broken bones to heal. The Latin name of *Uvularia* comes from the flowers, which were thought to resemble the uvula – the soft tissue hanging down the throat at the back of the palate.

FAMILY Lily
DESCRIPTION Spindly plant with an angled stem and sessile leaves, white or creamy-yellow hanging flowers on short stalks at the top of the stem
HABITAT Woodland; thickets
HEIGHT 6–12 ins (15–30 cm)
FLOWER Trumpet-shaped, 1¼ ins (3 cm) long
FLOWERING May–June
LEAVES Oblong, clasping, 2–3 ins (5–7.5 cm) long

CANADA VIOLET
(VIOLA CANADENSIS)

FAMILY Violet

DESCRIPTION Small woodland plant with heart-shaped leaves and several slender stalks bearing sweet-scented white flowers

HABITAT Shady deciduous woodland

HEIGHT 8–15 ins (20–38 cm)

FLOWER Irregular with two symmetrical halves, 1 in (2.5 cm) in diameter

FLOWERING April–July

LEAVES Cordate, finely toothed, 2–4 ins (5–10 cm) long

Canada Violet is a small woodland plant, with a cluster of long, heart-shaped leaves. The leaves are finely toothed and have quite long stalks. The fragrant flowers are borne on slender purple-green stalks and have the typical violet shape, with two upper petals and three lower. The petals are white, but the lower three are finely streaked with purple and are yellow at the base. Since it prefers cooler temperatures, Canada Violet thrives best in northern areas and at higher altitudes elsewhere, but will do well in a wildflower garden if positioned in a shady, cool area. The leaves and roots of this plant were once used as an emetic.

BEARGRASS;
(XEROPHYLLUM TENAX) INDIAN BASKET GRASS

Beargrass is an unusual and distinctive wildflower, with its many tiny, white flowers in a dense, cylindrical, and domed raceme cluster that looks a little like a bottle-brush. The individual flowers have six segments in a flat, open, star-like shape. The stout flower stalks spring from the center of a clump of leaves, which, as the second half of its common name might suggest, are rather grass-like – very long and narrow and growing in a tightly packed, massive clump. The alternative common name of Indian Basket Grass comes from American Indians having traditionally used the leaves to weave into baskets.

FAMILY Lily
DESCRIPTION Tall, dense, elongated, and rounded cluster of tiny white flowers, on a stout stalk springing from a large clump of basal leaves
HABITAT Open woods and clearings, often at higher altitude
HEIGHT 50–60 ins (125–150 cm)
FLOWER Elongated rounded cluster, 4–22 ins (10–55 cm) in length
FLOWERING June–August
LEAVES Basal, linear, 12–18 ins (30–75 cm) long

SOAPWEED YUCCA
(YUCCA GLAUCA)

FAMILY Agave
DESCRIPTION A basal rosette of rigid, sword-like leaves with hairy edges, and a tall stout stalk bearing an elongated cluster of bowl-shaped white flowers
HABITAT Plains
HEIGHT 24–48 ins (60–120 cm)
FLOWER Elongated cluster, each flower 1½ ins (3.75 cm)
FLOWERING May–July
LEAVES Basal rosette, linear, up to 24 ins (60 cm) long

Although it grows in such inhospitable areas, Soapweed Yucca is a large plant, with a basal rosette of long, linear, sword-like, gray-green leaves with sharply-pointed tips and hairy edges. The white flowers are bowl-shaped and hanging, held in a crowded elongated cluster on a single, stout stalk. Due to their dramatic tropical appearance, yuccas are often cultivated in gardens, and sometimes escape into the wild outside their traditional range. Modern research suggests the plant has antifungal, antitumor and antiarthritic properties. There are 30 species in this genus found in North America, most in the southwest desert.

JACK-IN-THE-PULPIT;
(ARISAEMA TRIPHYLLUM) INDIAN TURNIP

Jack-in-the-pulpit usually has only one or two leaves, which are each divided into three elliptical leaflets, and are set at the end of long stalks. The spathe curves over the top of the browny-yellow spadix and is green, streaked, and mottled with brown-purple. The spadix has male and female flowers hidden away at its base. The common name of Jack-in-the-pulpit comes from the spadix enclosed in the spathe, which resembles a person standing in a pulpit. The underground root is rather peppery and hot if eaten raw, but is quite palatable when cooked. A root tea was traditionally used as a purgative and to treat asthma, bronchitis, and colds.

FAMILY Arum
DESCRIPTION Upright, curved spathe around a browny-yellow spadix, with three-part green leaves
HABITAT Swamps; damp woods
HEIGHT 12–30 ins (30–75 cm)
FLOWER Cluster, 2–3 ins (5–7.5 cm) in length
FLOWERING April–June
LEAVES Tripartite, each leaflet elliptical, 1–2 ins (2.5–5 cm) long

CHOCOLATE LILY; MISSION BELLS; CHECKER LILY
(FRITILLARIA AFFINIS (FRITILLARIA LANCEOLATA))

FAMILY Lily

DESCRIPTION Small plant with long, lanceolate leaves on the upper stem and mottled browny-green, urn-shaped, pendant flowers

HABITAT Grassy meadows; open woods

HEIGHT 12–48 ins (30–120 cm)

FLOWER Pendant urn shape, ½–1 in (1.25–5 cm) long

FLOWERING March–June

LEAVES Lanceolate, whorled, up to 6 ins (15 cm) long

There is a great deal of confusion around this plant. *F. affinis* has been renamed, having previously been called *F. lanceolata*, and its common name of Chocolate Lily is also given to another member of the *Fritillaria* genus, *F. biflora*. Spotted Mountain Bells (*F. atropurpurea*) is also commonly called Checker Lily. The three species are all very similar, but *F. affinis* has mottled greenish-brown, bowl-shaped flowers on an erect stem, with long lanceolate leaves on the upper section of the stem. *F. biflora* has dark brown unmottled flowers and its leaves are on the lower part of the stem, and *F. atropurpurea* has smaller flowers and much longer, narrower leaves.

BROADLEAF CATTAIL;
(TYPHA LATIFOLIA) COMMON CATTAIL

Broadleaf Cattail is a tall plant, with long, stiff, linear leaves sheathing the stem. The slender flower spike has tiny yellowish male flowers at the top, with brown female flowers beneath. The flowers have bristles instead of sepals and petals; the female flowers have one pistil and the male three stamens. Broadleaf Cattail spreads quickly via creeping roots, and creates a good habitat for wildlife, but may be poisonous to grazing animals. American Indians made a poultice from the roots for wounds, sores, and burns, and used the fuzz from the female flowerhead to stop chafing in babies. There is only one genus in this family, with ten species found all round the world.

FAMILY Cattail

DESCRIPTION Tall water plant, with long, sword-like leaves and a cylindrical spike of tiny male flowers at the top of a much longer spike of brown, velvety female flowers

HABITAT Shallow water; freshwater marshes

HEIGHT 36–100 ins (90–260 cm)

FLOWER Elongated cluster, 6 ins (15 cm) in length

FLOWERING May–July

LEAVES Linear, sheathing, 2–8 ft (60–250 cm) long

SEA OATS
(UNIOLA PANICULATA)

Sea Oats is a very tall, eye-catching plant, with long, grass-like leaves and a tall, smooth stem that ends in a spectacular curving plume. The flowers forming the plume have no sepals or petals, but are made up of stamens and pistil enclosed in bracts, and grouped in brownish spikelets. Sea Oats is a native American wildflower and is a perennial that grows from a rhizome. It prefers to grow in full sun and will tolerate lack of water very well, so it prefers to grow on coastal sands and is quite often planted deliberately to control erosion on beaches. It should never be disturbed in the wild, as it is illegal to damage it. The similar but smaller Indian Wood Oats (*U. latifolium* or *Chasmanthium latifolium*) is an inland plant and has a much wider range across most of the southeast states, and is also sometimes planted as an ornamental grass in gardens or to be harvested for dried flower arrangements.

FAMILY Grass
DESCRIPTION Large, grass-like plant with curving elongated flower cluster at the top of a smooth stem
HABITAT Coastal sands
HEIGHT 30–84 ins (75–210 cm)
FLOWER Elongated cluster, 6–18 ins (15–45 cm) long
FLOWERING July
LEAVES Linear, grass-like, up to 16 in (40 cm) long

DESERT SAND VERBENA (ABRONIA VILLOSA)

FAMILY Four-o'clock
DESCRIPTION Low-growing, sticky-haired plant, with bright pinky-purple, trumpet-shaped flowers
HABITAT Sandy desert
HEIGHT Creeper, 6 ins (15 cm)
FLOWER Rounded cluster, 2–3 ins (5–8 cm) in diameter
FLOWERING March–October
LEAVES Opposite, ovate, scalloped, up to 1½ ins (2 cm) long

A low-growing, creeping plant, Desert Sand Verbena has long, trailing, reddish stems that can extend up to 36 ins (90 cm). They bear ovate, dark green leaves with slightly scalloped edges, in opposite pairs, and both leaves and stems are fleshy and covered with a fine layer of soft, sticky hairs. The flower stalks spring from the leaf axils, with rounded, almost spherical clusters of bright pink to purple-red, trumpet-shaped flowers. Sweet Sand Verbena (*A. fragrans*) is found in a similar area, but has sweet-smelling white flowers and is a more erect plant. There are 23 species in this genus found in North America, mostly in the west.

(AGROSTEMMA GITHAGO) CORNCOCKLE

A native of Europe, Corncockle has now spread across much of Canada and the United States, and is fully naturalized. It is a slender plant with stiffly erect leaves arranged in opposite pairs and bright pink, or sometimes white, flowers on the end of long stalks. Its branching stem is covered in fine white hairs. In England the Corncockle was once a common weed in grain fields and its poisonous seeds had to be manually picked out of harvested wheat, as bread made with contaminated wheat is quite capable of poisoning a human. Even today the plant remains a problem for farmers in grain-producing areas.

FAMILY Carnation
DESCRIPTION Tall, hairy plant, with bright pink flowers on long stalks
HABITAT Roadsides; disturbed soil
HEIGHT 12–36 ins (30–90 cm)
FLOWER Radially symmetrical, 1 in (2.5 cm) in diameter
FLOWERING June–September
LEAVES Narrowly-lanceolate, opposite, up to 4 ins (10 cm) long

NODDING ONION (ALLIUM CERNUUM)

FAMILY Lily

DESCRIPTION Basal cluster of long, narrow leaves, with an erect flower stalk curved at the top and bearing an umbel cluster of tiny pink or white flowers

HABITAT Open woodland

HEIGHT 12–24 ins (30–60 cm)

FLOWER Umbel cluster, each flower ¼ in (0.5 cm) long

FLOWERING July–August

LEAVES Basal, narrow and linear, 2–10 ins (5–25 cm) long

Nodding Onion has long, narrow, linear, and basal leaves, with a bare, slender, and arching stem that ends in a drooping umbel cluster of either pink or white flowers. Although it is closely related to and very similar to the Autumn Wild Onion (*A. stellatum*) Nodding Onion is differentiated because it flowers rather earlier in the year and the flowers are held in a drooping cluster, rather than erect, and also have a less lavender tint. Nodding Onion is a perennial that grows afresh each year from a bulb, which Cherokee Indians once used to treat colds, colic, and croup; a poultice of the whole plant was traditionally applied to the chest for respiratory ailments.

(ASCLEPIAS INCARNATA) SWAMP MILKWEED

Unlike many other milkweeds, Swamp Milkweed much prefers damp and swampy ground – but it looks very similar to the other species and has the same milky-white sap. It is a perennial plant with a smooth stem and many branches, bearing long, lanceolate leaves arranged in opposite pairs. The flowers are held in umbel clusters at the top of the stems, and are usually bright pink – although they may sometimes be white. Early American colonists used a tea made from the roots to treat asthma, rheumatism, and as a heart tonic, but it is now believed that the plant is potentially toxic so it should be used with some caution.

FAMILY Milkweed

DESCRIPTION Tall, branching plant with many long, narrow leaves and an umbel cluster of deep pink flowers

HABITAT Swamps; damp thickets; coastal areas

HEIGHT 12–48 ins (30–120 cm)

FLOWER Umbel cluster, each flower ½ in (0.5 cm) in diameter

FLOWERING June–August

LEAVES Lanceolate, opposite, up to 4 ins (10 cm) long

SHOWY MILKWEED (ASCLEPIAS SPECIOSA)

FAMILY Milkweed
DESCRIPTION Erect, leafy plant, with velvet-gray stems and rounded umbel clusters of star-shaped pink flowers
HABITAT Gravel slopes; dry areas; brush
HEIGHT 1–6 ft (30–180 cm)
FLOWER Rounded cluster, each flower ¾ in (2 cm) in diameter
FLOWERING June–August
LEAVES Oblong to ovate, large, opposite, 4–8 ins (10–20 cm) long

Showy Milkweed is a perennial that often spreads to form quite large clumps, and it is one of the most widely distributed species of milkweed. Although some are highly poisonous, Showy Milkweed is one of the non-toxic varieties. It is a velvety-gray plant, with a stout stem and long, large, oblong to ovate leaves arranged in opposite pairs. The sweet-scented flowers are pink and star-like, with five petals and five reddish sepals, and five erect hoods that curve inwards at the center. They are borne in dense, rounded umbel clusters, on short stalks that spring from the upper leaf axils, and at the top of the stem.

(ASCLEPIAS SYRIACA) COMMON MILKWEED

Common Milkweed is a tall perennial, with opposite, long, light green leaves – downy gray beneath – and rather drooping globe-shaped clusters of pinky-purple flowers. The leaves exude a milky-white sap when bruised, hence its common name. Milkweed foliage is the only food of Monarch butterfly larvae, and the toxic sap makes both the larvae and the adult butterfly poisonous to predators. Despite this, the plant had a wide range of medicinal uses for early Americans, including wart removal, and as a laxative and contraceptive. Its silky seed tassels were also used to stuff pillows and mattresses.

FAMILY Milkweed

DESCRIPTION Tall, downy plant with large oblong or oval leaves, pinky-purple flowers in a rather drooping umbel cluster

HABITAT Roadsides; fields; waste ground

HEIGHT 2–6 ft (60–180 cm)

FLOWER Rounded umbel cluster, 2 ins (5 cm) in width

FLOWERING June–August

LEAVES Large, oblong or oval, 4–10 ins (10–25 cm) long

SAGEBRUSH MARIPOSA LILY

(CALOCHORTUS MACROCARPUS)

Sagebrush Mariposa Lily is one of the most common sagebrush lilies across the northwest. It has a rather stout, straight stem, with several long, narrow leaves arranged alternately along its length. The leaves are dark green and often turn up at the very tip. The attractive bell-shaped flowers appear roughly triangular when seen from above, with three broad, fan-like petals and three long, narrow, pointed sepals. They are borne in a loose umbel cluster and there is usually a maximum of three flowers on each stem. The petals are pink to lavender, with a whitish oblong gland at the base of each; the line where the two colors join is fringed, with a deeper pink to lilac crescent mark above. There is also a white form with a red stripe on each petal, which only occurs in an area around southeast Washington and western Idaho.

FAMILY Lily

DESCRIPTION Erect, stout-stemmed plant with linear leaves and several bell-shaped pinky-lilac flowers in a loose cluster

HABITAT Dry soil sagebrush; coniferous forest

HEIGHT 9–22 ins (22–55 cm)

FLOWER Radially symmetrical, 1–2½ ins (2.5–6.25 cm) in diameter

FLOWERING May–August

LEAVES Linear, narrow, 2–4 ins (5–10 cm) long

CUTLEAF TOOTHWORT
(CARDAMINE CONCATENATA (DENTARIA LACINATA))

FAMILY Mustard

DESCRIPTION Small plant with three deeply-lobed and toothed leaves in a whorl around the middle of the stem and terminal clusters of small white or pink flowers

HABITAT Moist woodland

HEIGHT 9–15 ins (22–38 cm)

FLOWER Terminal cluster, each flower ¾ in (2 cm) in diameter

FLOWERING April–June

LEAVES Tripalmate, sharply-toothed, whorled, 2–5 ins (5–12.5 cm) wide

Cutleaf Toothwort was previously placed in a totally different genus, and had the scientific name of *Dentaria lacinata*. It is an attractive woodland plant, with lanceolate and sharply-toothed, tripalmate leaves. They are usually seen arranged in whorls of three just above the midpoint of the stem, but there are also basal leaves that are only evident before the plant begins to flower. The pretty four-petaled flowers are borne in a small terminal cluster and can be either pink or white. The root has tooth-shaped projections – hence the plant's common name – and quite a peppery taste; it can be added to salads or made into a tasty relish.

PIPSISSEWA
(CHIMAPHILA UMBELLATA)

Pipsissewa is a small plant, with shiny dark green, lanceolate, toothed leaves arranged in whorls and pink-white flowers in a small drooping cluster at the end of a bare stem. An evergreen perennial, it is found in dry woodland. American Indians used a tea of the leaves to treat backache, kidney and bladder problems, and as an astringent. Early doctors also used the plant for urinary problems. Recent scientific testing has confirmed it has diuretic, antiseptic and antibacterial properties. Spotted Wintergreen (*C. maculata*) is very similar, but it has spotted leaves and is not found in the west, although its range does extend further down into the south.

FAMILY Wintergreen
DESCRIPTION Low-growing plant with shiny, dark green whorled leaves and several pink flowers in small clusters at the top of the stem
HABITAT Dry woodland
HEIGHT 6–12 ins (15–30 cm)
FLOWER Radially symmetrical, ½ in (1.25 cm) in diameter
FLOWERING June–August
LEAVES Lanceolate, toothed, whorled, ¾–2½ ins (2–6.5 cm) long

FAREWELL-TO-SPRING
(CLARKIA AMOENA)

Farewell-to-spring varies quite widely in height, but is generally a slender, open plant with long lanceolate green leaves and fairly small bowl-shaped flowers. The flower has four broad, fan-shaped petals that are shiny pale pink with a deeper pink to purple, rectangular to triangular blotch towards the base. The flowers are borne in a loose cluster, and they open during the day and remain closed at night. Since it only comes into flower as spring turns into summer, Farewell-to-spring is very aptly named. It prefers to grow on well-drained ground, on dry, grassy slopes and in clearings in woodland or brush. There are around 30 species in this genus in North America, almost all in California and its immediate neighboring states. The Latin name of the genus honors Captain William Clark, who traveled to the Northwest frontier with Meriwether Lewis in 1806.

FAMILY Evening-primrose
DESCRIPTION Slender, open plant, with pink, bowl-shaped flowers in a loose cluster
HABITAT Dry slopes; brushy woodland clearings
HEIGHT 8–34 ins (20–85 cm)
FLOWER Radially symmetrical, 1–1½ ins (2.5–3.75 cm)
FLOWERING June–August
LEAVES Lanceolate, 1–3 ins (2.5–7.5 cm) long

RED RIBBONS
(CLARKIA CONCINNA)

FAMILY Evening-primrose
DESCRIPTION Low-growing, branching plant, with many broad, elliptical leaves and showy, bright pink flowers thickly clustered from leaf axils
HABITAT Shady mountain slopes
HEIGHT 8–12 ins (20–30 cm)
FLOWER Rounded cluster, each flower 1–2 ins (2.5–5 cm) in diameter
FLOWERING May–June
LEAVES Broadly elliptical, ½–2 ins (1.25–5 cm) in length

Red Ribbons is a very attractive, low-growing plant with branching stems bearing many broad, elliptical leaves. The rather complex-looking, showy bright pink flowers spring from the leaf axils, growing in thick clusters. They have four narrow petals that flare widely towards the tip, where they are deeply divided into three spreading lobes. In Red Ribbons the three lobes are all roughly the same width, but in the very similar but taller species Beautiful Clarkia (*C. pulchella*) the central lobe is noticeably longer and wider than the other two. Beautiful Clarkia grows in more open ground and its range spreads further north and east.

CAROLINA SPRING BEAUTY

(CLAYTONIA CAROLINIANA)

Carolina Spring Beauty is a low-growing plant with broad, ovate, dark green leaves, which are arranged in opposite pairs clasping the stem. The rounded shape of the leaves distinguish it from the otherwise rather similar-looking Spring Beauty (*C. virginica*) which grows in roughly the same range and habitat, but has linear leaves. The attractive flowers of Carolina Spring Beauty are quite small, with five pink or pinky-white petals striped with a deeper pink and borne in a loose, terminal raceme cluster. As its common name suggests, Carolina Spring Beauty is spring-flowering and makes lovely patches of bright color early in the year.

FAMILY Purslane

DESCRIPTION Low-growing plant, with dark green ovate leaves and loose terminal raceme clusters of small, pink flowers

HABITAT Damp, open woodland; garden lawns

HEIGHT 6–16 ins (15–40 cm)

FLOWER Radially symmetrical, ½–¾ in (1.25–2 cm) in diameter

FLOWERING March–May

LEAVES Ovate, 2–6 ins (5–15 cm) long

ROCKY MOUNTAIN BEE PLANT
(CLEOME SERRULATA)

FAMILY Caper
DESCRIPTION Bushy, branching plant with tripalmate leaves and rounded raceme clusters of small pink flowers at the tip of the branches
HABITAT Mountain foothills; rangelands
HEIGHT 9–60 ins (22–150 cm)
FLOWER Rounded cluster, each flower ½ in (1.25 cm) in length
FLOWERING July–September
LEAVES Tripalmate, leaflets lanceolate ½–2 ins (1.25–5 cm) long

The sweet nectar of Rocky Mountain Bee Plant attracts bees, hence its common name. It is a branching, bushy plant, each branch bearing many alternate tripalmate leaves with long, lanceolate, and dark green leaflets. The lower leaves have short stalks, the upper leaves are nearly sessile. The stems terminate in loose raceme clusters of pink to lavender flowers – occasionally they are white. The flowers have four long, narrow petals and six even longer stamens, so the overall effect is of a softly spiky, slightly elongated globe. The long seed pods are borne on the end of short stalks, and appear lower down the raceme when the top is still in flower.

DEPTFORD PINK
(DIANTHUS ARMERIA)

A native of Europe, Deptford Pink was introduced to North America and is now found across much of the continent. It is named for Deptford in England, where it was once found in great numbers. It has a tall, stiff, erect stem, which is smooth and slender but noticeably swollen at each leaf node. The long, thin, opposite leaves are dark green. The flowers are bright pink, often with white spots, and resemble very simple carnations — the plant comes from the same family — and are borne in a loose cluster on the tips of the stems. There are several varieties of Pink growing wild in North America, many of which have escaped from gardens.

FAMILY Carnation

DESCRIPTION Medium-size plant with stiff erect stems, swollen at the leaf nodes, and a terminal cluster of bright pink flowers

HABITAT Roadsides; dry fields

HEIGHT 6–24 ins (15–60 cm)

FLOWER Radially symmetrical, ½ in (1.25 cm) in diameter

FLOWERING May–September

LEAVES Thin and grass-like, opposite, erect, 1–4 ins (2.5–10 cm) in length

WILD BLEEDING HEART

(DICENTRA EXIMIA)

Wild Bleeding Heart is an attractive, branching perennial with several long, feathery, leaves springing from the base of the plant. The leaves are blue-green in color, pinnately compound and divided and with lobed leaflets. The deep pink flowers are borne in a loose, branching raceme cluster at the end of a bare stalk. Each flower is shaped rather like a bleeding heart, with the two outer petals forming the heart and the inner two protruding at the base to look like a drop of blood. Wild Bleeding Heart is a native North American wildflower, but there is also a very similar Asian species, Asian Bleeding Heart (*D. Spectabilis*), which is cultivated in gardens in many areas and has escaped to the wild, where it has spread. Asian Bleeding Heart can be distinguished by its rather larger and showier flowers.

FAMILY Fumitory
DESCRIPTION Branching plant with long, blue-green, pinnately-divided leaves and drooping clusters of heart-shaped pink flowers
HABITAT Rocky woodland
HEIGHT 12–18 ins (30–45 cm)
FLOWER Heart-shaped, ¾ in (2 cm) long
FLOWERING May–September
LEAVES Basal, pinnately compound, divided, 1–4 ins (2.5–10 cm) long

SEASIDE DAISY
(ERIGERON GLAUCUS)

FAMILY Aster

DESCRIPTION Low-growing plant with basal rosette of leaves, cluster of bristly, sticky stems each bearing a pink, daisy-like flower

HABITAT Coastal bluffs; dunes

HEIGHT 6–18 ins (15–45 cm)

FLOWER Compound flower head, 2½ ins (6.25 cm) in diameter

FLOWERING April–July

LEAVES Basal rosette, spatulate, sometimes toothed, up to 5 ins (12.5 cm) long

There are over 140 species in this genus found across North America, but some of them are unattractive weeds. Seaside Daisy is unusual in that it is a slightly succulent plant, probably due to its prefered habitat near the sea. It has a basal rosette of long, spatulate leaves that narrow to a flat stalk at the base and are often toothed toward the tip. The pretty, daisy-like compound flower heads are made up of very many short, slender, pale pink to white ray florets, surrounding a central yellow disk. The flower heads are borne at the end of short, bristly, sticky-haired stalks, with several on each plant.

COMMON FLEABANE;
PHILADELPHIA FLEABANE;
(ERIGERON PHILADELPHICUS) DAISY FLEABANE

A slim, branching plant, Common Fleabane has long, spatulate lower leaves and smaller, clasping upper leaves that are often toothed or lobed. The flower heads are borne at the end of long, branching stalks, often with several found on each plant. They have many slender, pinky-white ray florets, around a large yellow central disk. A tea brewed from Common Fleabane was a traditional remedy for diarrhea, kidney stones, and to stop hemorrhages. It was also used to treat fevers, bronchitis, and coughs. However, it should not be collected or used medicinally without expert guidance as touching the plant can sometimes lead to contact dermatitis.

FAMILY Aster

DESCRIPTION Leafy plant with some long hairs, upper stem branching, small compound flowers with white rays and yellow central disk

HABITAT Open moist woodland; fields; overgrown places

HEIGHT 6–24 ins (15–45 cm)

FLOWER Compound flower head, ½–1 in (1.25–2.5 cm) in diameter

FLOWERING April–July

LEAVES Lower, spatulate, up to 6 ins (15 cm) long, tapering to a stalk; upper, toothed, clasping

TEXAS STORKSBILL
(ERODIUM TEXANUM)

FAMILY Geranium
DESCRIPTION A low-growing, trailing plant, with reddish hairy stems and small pinky-purple flowers in a loose cluster
HABITAT Prairies; deserts
HEIGHT Creeper, 6 ins (15 cm)
FLOWER Radially symmetrical, 1 in (2.5 cm) in diameter
FLOWERING February–June
LEAVES Ovate, three lobes, up to 4 ins (10 cm) long

Texas Storksbill is a native North American wildflower, part of the *Geranium* family. It is a low-growing, trailing plant but it can have horizontal stems up to 20 ins (50 cm) in length. The stems are reddish in color and roughly hairy and the leaves are generally ovate with three rather rounded lobes, the edges of which are also bluntly toothed. The pink flowers have five rounded petals, five sepals and a cluster of ten stamens, and are borne in a loose cluster. There are nine species in this genus found in North America, including Storksbill (*E. cicutarium*), which has become naturalized from Europe and has smaller flowers and fern-like leaves.

COMMON JOE-PYE WEED; HOLLOW JOE-PYE WEED TRUMPETWEED;
(EUPATORIUM FISTULOSUM)

Joe-Pye Weed gets its very unusual common name from an old folklore tradition that a nineteenth-century American called Joe Pye used it to cure typhus fever. There are several very similar-looking species across the east, but Common Joe-Pye Weed has a sturdy hollow stem with a whitish bloom, bearing whorls of long, lanceolate and blunt-toothed leaves. It can be distinguished by the leaves, which have a single main vein — unlike other species in the genus, which have three main veins. At the top of the tall, sturdy stem is a flat-topped cluster of tiny, fuzzy-looking pinky-purple flowers.

FAMILY Aster
DESCRIPTION Large plant with a tall hollow stem bearing long lanceolate leaves with a single main vein and topped with a flat cluster of pink-purple flowers
HABITAT Damp fields and meadows; coastal areas
HEIGHT 2–6 ft (60–180 cm)
FLOWER Flat-topped cluster, 4–6 ins (10–15 cm) wide
FLOWERING July–September
LEAVES Lanceolate, toothed, whorled, 2–8 ins (5–20 cm) long

SPOTTED JOE-PYE WEED
(EUPATORIUM MACULATUM)

The most distinctive feature of Spotted Joe-Pye Weed is its sturdy stem, which is either deep purple or green thickly spotted with purple; other species in the genus generally have green stems with only a small amount of purple spotting. The stem bears whorls of long, lanceolate and sharply-toothed leaves on short stalks. The rather fuzzy-looking, branching flower cluster is at the top of the stem, and has a flat top. American Indians used a tea made from the whole plant as a diuretic, and a tea made from the root to treat a variety of ailments, including fevers, colds, diarrhea, liver and kidney ailments, and rheumatism. Other similar species of this genus in the same area include Hollow Joe-Pye Weed (*E. fistulosum* – see page 187), which has a hollow greenish stem and is slightly smaller.

FAMILY Aster
DESCRIPTION Large plant with a tall, purple-spotted stem bearing long lanceolate leaves with three main veins and topped with a flat cluster of pink-purple flowers
HABITAT Damp fields and meadows; coastal areas
HEIGHT 2–7 ft (60–210 cm)
FLOWER Flat-topped cluster, 4–6 ins (10–15 cm) wide
FLOWERING July–September
LEAVES Lanceolate, toothed, whorled, 2–8 ins (5–20 cm) long

CRANESBILL (GERANIUM CAROLINIANUM)

FAMILY Geranium

DESCRIPTION Low-growing annual, with palmate, lobed and deeply-toothed leaves and a compact cluster of small pink flowers

HABITAT Rocky woodland

HEIGHT 6–20 ins (15–50 cm)

FLOWER Radially symmetrical, ¼–½ in (0.5–1.25 cm) in diameter

FLOWERING April–June

LEAVES Palmate, deeply-toothed lobes, up to 5 ins (12.5 cm) long

An annual wildflower, Cranesbill has a branching stem and palmate leaves with five deeply-toothed lobes. The basal leaves have fairly long stalks, but those higher up the stem are usually much shorter. The small flowers are very pale pink or lavender, with five rounded petals, and are borne in small raceme clusters at the end of the branches. The name Cranesbill comes from the fruit, which is elongated and shaped like a beak. The very similar Bicknell's Cranes Bill (*G. bicknelli*) is found in the same general area, but has smaller flowers with notched petals, which are borne in a looser cluster.

(GERANIUM MACULATUM) WILD GERANIUM

Another member of the *Geranium* family, Wild Geranium is a perennial found in woodland across the northeast. A fairly low-growing plant, it has a branching stem and many palmate leaves, each with five deeply-toothed lobes. The basal leaves have longer stalks than those higher up the stem. The pink, lavender – or occasionally white – flowers have five rounded petals and are borne in very loose raceme clusters of a just few flowers at the end of the branches. In folk medicine, the root of Wild Geranium was used to treat cancer, stop bleeding and diarrhea, and for kidney and stomach problems.

FAMILY Geranium
DESCRIPTION Perennial, branching plant, with palmate, lobed and deeply-toothed leaves and a loose cluster of small pink flowers
HABITAT Woodland; thickets
HEIGHT 12–24 ins (30–60 cm)
FLOWER Radially symmetrical, 1–2 ins (2.5–5 cm) in diameter
FLOWERING April–June
LEAVES Palmate, deeply-toothed lobes, 4–5 ins (10–12.5 cm) long

STICKY GERANIUM
(GERANIUM VISCOSISSIMUM)

In the west there are several very similar geraniums to be found, and it is often very difficult to identify the exact species by observation alone. Sticky Geranium has a hairy, branching stem, and palmate leaves on long stalks. The leaves are deeply incised into five – or sometimes seven – segments with toothed edges. Most of the branches carry a sparse cluster of small pinky-purple flowers at the top. Where it likes the conditions this species can be very common, turning the meadows pink in spring to early summer. The genus name *Geranium* is derived from the Greek word for crane, because the fruit resembles its bill, and more than one species is commonly known as Crane's Bill. Richardson's Geranium (*G. richardsonii*) also grows in a similar area, but usually has pinky-white flowers that appear slightly later in June.

FAMILY Geranium
DESCRIPTION Hairy-stemmed plant, with many branches and palmate and segmented leaves with long stalks, small pinky-purple flowers in a sparse open cluster
HABITAT Open meadows; woodland clearings
HEIGHT 12–36 ins (30–90 cm)
FLOWER Radially symmetrical, 1 in (2.5 cm) in diameter
FLOWERING May–July
LEAVES Palmate, deeply incised into segments, toothed, up to 5 ins (12.5 cm) wide

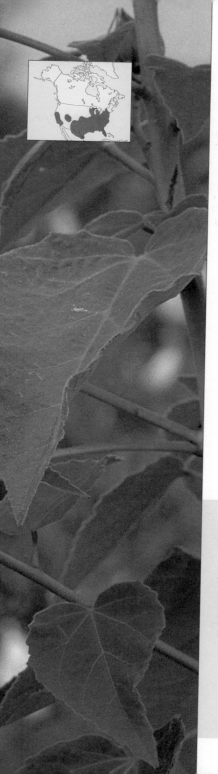

CRIMSON-EYED ROSEMALLOW; SWAMP ROSEMALLOW

(HIBISCUS MOSCHEUTOS (HIBISCUS PALUSTRIS))

A tall, showy plant, Crimson-eyed Rosemallow has a coarse stem with long, ovate to lanceolate, pointed leaves that are toothed or lobed. The leaves are a yellowy-green in color with soft white hairs on the underside. The large, attractive, bowl-shaped flowers have five broad lobes and are usually white or pink, but can be a deep purple-red in the center. They have many stamens, are strongly musk-scented and are borne at the end of short stalks springing from the leaf axils. As well as salt water marshes, Crimson-eyed Rosemallow thrives in very wet, inland areas, even on the uplands. The leaves and roots were once used to treat dysentery, and lung and urinary ailments.

FAMILY Mallow

DESCRIPTION Tall plant with yellow-green, ovate to lanceolate leaves on a coarse stem, large pinky-white flowers with a darker center borne on short stalks from the leaf axils

HABITAT Tidal marshes; swamps

HEIGHT 30–84 ins (75–210 cm)

FLOWER Radially symmetrical, 4–8 ins (10–20 cm)

FLOWERING June–September

LEAVES Ovate to lanceolate, toothed or lobed, 4 ins (10 cm) in length

BUSH MORNING GLORY
(IPOMOEA LEPTOPHYLLA)

FAMILY Morning Glory
DESCRIPTION Leafy-stemmed plant, mostly erect but sometimes with trailing branches, funnel-shaped deep pink to purple-red flowers
HABITAT Prairies; dry, sandy soil
HEIGHT 3–4 ft (90–120 cm)
FLOWER Radially symmetrical, 2–2½ ins (5–6.25 cm) in diameter
FLOWERING May–August
LEAVES Lanceolate, narrow, up to 3½ ins (9 cm) long

Bush Morning Glory has a smooth stem, with many long, narrow lanceolate leaves on quite short stalks. The attractive, funnel-shaped flowers are deep pink to purple-red in color, often becoming darker towards the center. They are borne on short stalks springing from the leaf axils on the upper part of the plant. Unlike cultivated morning glories, Bush Morning Glory is not a vine but a more or less erect plant – although sometimes the lower part of the plant does lean on the ground. Bush Morning Glory is related to the Wild Potato Vine (*I. pandurata*) and both these species are edible – the roots are boiled or baked like sweet potatoes.

RAILROAD VINE;
(IPOMOEA PES-CAPRAE) GOAT'S-HOOF VINE

Originally from West India, Railroad Vine was introduced to North America and has become naturalized across the warm areas of the continent – and in other warm areas of the world. It is a vine with a long stem that creeps across beaches and dunes, almost to the water's edge, rooting at the nodes. The stem bears long, broadly ovate, bright green leaves, which are folded at the center and deeply notched at the tip. Their shape resembles a goat's hoofprint, leading to the alternative common name of Goat's-hoof Vine. The flower stalks stand erect off the stem, bearing a pink to purple-red, funnel-shaped flower.

FAMILY Morning Glory

DESCRIPTION Vine with trailing stems, ovate leaves folded in the center and pinky-red funnel-shaped flowers

HABITAT Beaches; coastal dunes

HEIGHT Vine, stems up to 20 ft (600 cm) long

FLOWER Radially symmetrical, 2 ins (5 cm) in diameter

FLOWERING All year

LEAVES Broadly ovate, folded at the center, up to 4 ins (10 cm) long

HENBIT; COMMON DEAD NETTLE
(LAMIUM AMPLEXICAULE)

FAMILY Mint

DESCRIPTION Square-stemmed plant with whorled clusters of pinky-lavender flowers spring from the axils of the upper, scalloped leaves

HABITAT Fields; waste ground; roadsides

HEIGHT 5–18 ins (12.5–45 cm)

FLOWER Rounded cluster, each flower ½–¾ in (1.25–2 cm) across

FLOWERING March–November

LEAVES Ovate, scalloped, up to 1½ ins (3.75 cm) long; upper sessile and clasping; lower with long stalks

Henbit was originally a native European wildflower but was introduced to North America and is now fully naturalized across most of the continent. It has pink-lavender flowers that are arranged in a whorl around a rather squarish stem, in the axils of the upper sessile and clasping leaves. The lower leaves are a little larger, with quite long stalks and arranged in opposite pairs. The young leaves can be added to salads, and the tips dried and used as an herb for cooking. Two other similar species were also introduced from Europe, Spotted Henbit (*L. maculatum*) and Red Henbit (*L. purpureum*).

BITTERROOT
(LEWISIA REDIVIVA)

Bitterroot is the state flower of Montana. It is a small and very low-growing plant, with — for its size — comparatively large and very showy pink to white flowers. There are usually several flowers growing on a single plant, each with many long, lanceolate petals. The flowers are borne at the end of a short stalk and grow within a basal rosette of long, linear, and succulent leaves. There are 15 other species in this genus to be found across North America. Bitterroot is a species that prefers drier soil, and it is commonly found growing in open pinewoods, and also in sagebrush areas.

FAMILY Purslane
DESCRIPTION Low-growing plant with basal rosette of succulent leaves and large, showy pink flowers
HABITAT Open coniferous woods; sagebrush areas
HEIGHT 2 ins (5 cm)
FLOWER Radially symmetrical, 1½–2 ins (3.75–5 cm) in diameter
FLOWERING May–July
LEAVES Succulent basal rosette, each leaf up to 2 ins (5 cm) long

DOTTED BLAZING STAR; DOTTED GAYFEATHER
(LIATRIS PUNCTATA)

There are 34 species in this genus found across North America, mostly in the center or in the east of the continent. Dotted Blazing Star is a tall, erect perennial with several stems, each bearing many long, narrow leaves along its length. The leaves are bright green marked with tiny, resinous dots, hence the plant's common name, and stand stiffly rather than drooping. The rather shaggy-looking, pinky-purple flower heads are each made up of four to six disk flowers and are arranged in a dense, narrow, elongated spike at the end of each stem. A tea made from the roots of this and other *Liatris* species was a folk remedy for kidney and bladder problems, and was used as a gargle for sore throats.

FAMILY Aster
DESCRIPTION Tall, leafy plant, with several stems bearing narrow, thickly-clustered pinky-purple flowers in an elongated cluster
HABITAT Plains; open, dry ground; among piñon and juniper
HEIGHT 8–32 ins (20–80 cm)
FLOWER Elongated cluster, each flower ¾ in (2 cm) in length
FLOWERING August–September
LEAVES Narrow, dotted, up to 6 ins (15 cm) long

PRAIRIE BLAZING STAR
(LIATRIS PYCNOSTACHYA)

FAMILY Aster

DESCRIPTION Coarse plant with a leafy, hairy stem ending in a dense spike of rose-purple flowers

HABITAT Damp areas of prairies

HEIGHT 22–72 ins (55–180 cm)

FLOWER Spike of densely-clustered flower heads, each flower ¾ in (1.25 cm) in diameter

FLOWERING July–September

LEAVES Linear, with translucent dots, up to 12 ins (30 cm) long

Prairie Blazing Star is a very tall perennial plant with a coarse, hairy stem that has many rough, linear leaves covered with translucent dots. The shaggy-looking flower heads, which are normally rose-purple – although sometimes there is an odd white one – are made up of 5–12 sessile florets, and are borne on a crowded spike. As well as being a well-known wildflower, Prairie Blazing Star is also often cultivated as a popular garden plant. Devil's Bit (*Chamaelirium luteum*) is also sometimes called Blazing Star, but it looks quite different as it has a spike of white flowers and leaves in a basal rosette.

DENSE BLAZING STAR;
(LIATRIS SPICATA) GAY FEATHER

Dense Blazing Star is a very tall plant, and the lower part of the stem has numerous alternate and very long, linear leaves, which get progressively shorter the higher they are. The tall flower spike at the top of the stem is very densely covered in sessile, bright rose-purple flowers that have a rather feathery look due to the long styles that extend well beyond the petals – hence the plant's alternative common name. Dense Blazing Star prefers to grow on damp, low-lying ground so it is often found in damp meadows and in moist areas of the prairie.

FAMILY Aster

DESCRIPTION Tall, leafy-stemmed plant, with a long spike of feathery, rose-purple flowers

HABITAT Damp meadows; prairies

HEIGHT 1–6 ft (30–180 cm)

FLOWER Spike, each flower head ¼ in (0.5 cm) in width

FLOWERING July–September

LEAVES Linear, up to 12 ins (30 cm) in length

TWINFLOWER (LINNAEA BOREALIS)

FAMILY Honeysuckle
DESCRIPTION Creeping plant with erect forked stalk bearing two small trumpet-shaped pink flowers
HABITAT Bogs; shady woodland
HEIGHT Creeper, 4 ins (10 cm)
FLOWER Trumpet-shaped, ½ in (1.25 cm) in length
FLOWERING June–July
LEAVES Rounded elliptical, toothed, opposite, 1 in (2.5 cm) long

Twinflower is a delicate wildflower with long stems that trail along the ground and upright stalks of 3–6 ins (8–15 cm) that terminate in a fork, each side bearing a single flower. The sweet-smelling, pale pinky-white flowers are trumpet-shaped and hairy inside. The bright green leaves are shaped in a rounded ellipse, with shallow teeth and are arranged in opposite pairs low down on the stem. Although there is also a European variety of this species, Twinflower is a native American plant and is now relatively rare so should not be picked or removed from its natural habitat in the wild. However, it is also often cultivated in wildflower gardens.

(MENTHA ARVENSIS) WILD MINT; FIELD MINT

Wild Mint is the only species of mint that is native to North America. When it is crushed, the plant smells strongly of mint and can be used as a flavoring. It is a branching plant, with a square, hairy stem and flowers held in rounded clusters whorled around in the upper leaf axils – most other species in this genus have flowers at the tip of the stem or on short stalks. The flowers normally range from pale pink through to lavender, although they are occasionally white. They have long stamens, making them look rather feathery. The leaves are long and lanceolate, with sharply-toothed edges, and are arranged in opposite pairs along the stem.

FAMILY Mint

DESCRIPTION Branching plant scented with mint, opposite toothed leaves and whorls of pink flowers round the stem in leaf axils

HABITAT Damp soil; stream edges

HEIGHT 6–30 ins (15–75 cm)

FLOWER Rounded cluster, each flower ¼ in (0.5 cm) in length

FLOWERING July–August

LEAVES Lanceolate, sharply toothed, 1–3 ins (2.5–7.5 cm) long

VIRGINIA BLUEBELLS;
VIRGINIA COWSLIP (MERTENSIA VIRGINICA)

FAMILY Borage

DESCRIPTION Grayish, toothed basal leaves, smaller and elliptical higher up. Loose, drooping clusters of trumpet-shaped pale blue flowers.

HABITAT Wet woodland; flood plains

HEIGHT 8–30 ins (20–75 cm)

FLOWER Loose cyme cluster, each flower 1 in (2.5 cm) in length

FLOWERING March–May

LEAVES Basal, toothed, up to 8 ins (20 cm) long; stem, smaller and elliptical

Virginia Bluebells is a quite large, erect plant, with long, toothed basal leaves and smaller, smooth-edged elliptical ones higher up the stem. Both types of leaf are smooth-surfaced but strongly veined and with a grayish bloom. The showy, trumpet-shaped flowers are borne in loose, drooping cyme clusters. They start off a delicate pale pink when in bud, becoming a very light blue as they open into flower. Virginia Bluebells tends to grow in massed clumps, forming great beds that can look spectacular when in full bloom. It is also sometimes cultivated in gardens, but needs very damp soil to thrive.

PINK MONKEYFLOWER; LEWIS'S MONKEYFLOWER
(MIMULUS LEWISII)

Pink Monkeyflower is quite a tall plant and its large, showy, pink flowers make it one of the most attractive and noticeable of mountain wildflowers. It has several branching stems covered in a fine layer of sticky hairs, with many long, ovate leaves arranged in opposite pairs. The leaves are sessile and toothed and also covered in fine sticky hairs. The flowers are irregular in two symmetrical halves, with three lobes curving downwards and two curving upwards. They are deep pink, with a patch of yellow hairs and darker red fine streaks on the central lower lobe. The bright color of the flowers attracts hummingbirds in the summer season to pollinate the plant.

FAMILY Figwort

DESCRIPTION Leafy plant with many stems bearing elliptical, toothed leaves springing straight from the stem, showy deep pink flowers

HABITAT Damp open ground at high altitude

HEIGHT 14–18 ins (35–120 cm)

FLOWER Irregular with two symmetrical halves, 1–2 ins (2.5–5 cm) long

FLOWERING June–August

LEAVES Elliptical, toothed, sessile, arranged in opposite pairs, 1–4 ins (2.5–10 cm) long

WILD BERGAMOT
(MONARDA FISTULOSA)

Wild Bergamot is a very showy perennial, and is often cultivated both in wildflower gardens and in herb gardens. It has a single, square, erect stem, often quite tall, bearing opposite pairs of gray-green leaves, which are lanceolate and toothed. The stem terminates in a dense, round cluster of pink to lavender flowers. The individual flowers are quite long with two lips, the upper with two lobes and the lower with three. Beneath the flower head there is a cluster of leaf-like bracts, which are pale green, often tinted with pink. The leaves of Wild Bergamot are aromatic and can be used to make mint tea. American Indians made a tea from them to treat colic and flatulence and early physicians also used a similar concoction to expel gas and worms. The essential oil has been scientifically proved to have anesthetic, anti-inflammatory, worm-expelling and antioxidant properties.

FAMILY Mint
DESCRIPTION Perennial plant with a single tall, square stem, bearing toothed, opposite leaves and a dense, showy cluster of pink to lavender flowers
HABITAT Dry, open ground
HEIGHT 2–5 ft (50–150 cm)
FLOWER Rounded cluster, each flower 1 in (2.5 cm) long
FLOWERING July–August
LEAVES Lanceolate, toothed, arranged in opposite pairs, 2 ins (5 cm) long

SHOWY EVENING-PRIMROSE
(OENOTHERA SPECIOSA)

FAMILY Evening-primrose
DESCRIPTION Downy-stemmed plant with many long, elliptical leaves and large, pink or pinky-white flowers
HABITAT Prairies; plains; waste ground
HEIGHT 9–26 ins (22–65 cm)
FLOWER Radially symmetrical, 1–3 ins (2.5–7.5 cm)
FLOWERING May–July
LEAVES Elliptical, with waved or cleft edges, 2–3 ins (5–7.5 cm) long

Showy Evening-primrose is a medium-size plant, with several slender, softly hairy stems bearing a great many elliptical leaves with wavy or cleft edges. When the buds appear they are rather drooping, but they open into quite large pink or white flowers, borne on short stalks that spring from the leaf axils. The four broad, rounded petals are often delicately veined with a deeper shade of pink, and have a touch of yellow at the base. This attractive plant is often grown in gardens, from where it escapes to the wild. Being very drought-resistant it can soon spread across quite large areas, creating an extensive display of color when it is in flower.

SALTMARSH FLEABANE
(PLUCHEA ODORATA (PLUCHEA PURPURASCENS))

When it is in bloom, the bright pink flowers of Saltmarsh Fleabane can be quite conspicuous amidst the dull browns and greens of marsh grasses. It is an erect plant with a smooth stem, bearing lanceolate, bright green leaves that are sometimes toothed or scalloped. The leaves may have short stalks, or are sometimes sessile, and are arranged alternately along the stem. The flower heads are held in small, flat-topped clusters, and have no ray florets, only disk florets. They are pinky-lavender in color, and smell very strongly of camphor. There are around six herbaceous species in this genus, found across North America.

FAMILY Aster

DESCRIPTION Tall, erect, smooth-stemmed plant with flat-topped clusters of pinky-lavender flower heads without rays, smells strongly of camphor

HABITAT Salt water marshes

HEIGHT 15–48 ins (38–120 cm)

FLOWER Rounded cluster, each flower head ¼ in (0.5 cm) in diameter

FLOWERING June–October

LEAVES Lanceolate, sometimes toothed or scalloped along the edges, up to 6 ins (15 cm) in length

VIRGINIA MEADOW BEAUTY; DEERGRASS
(RHEXIA VIRGINICA)

FAMILY Meadow Beauty

DESCRIPTION Medium-size plant with an almost oblong stem bearing ovate leaves and several small, bright pink flowers in terminal clusters

HABITAT Sandy swamps

HEIGHT 6–28 ins (15–70 cm)

FLOWER Radially symmetrical, 1–1½ ins (2.5–3.75 cm) in diameter

FLOWERING July–September

LEAVES Ovate to elliptical, toothed, up to 2½ ins (6.25 cm) long

Virginia Meadow Beauty is a small to medium size plant, with elliptical, toothed leaves arranged in opposite pairs along the rather oblong-shaped stem. The leaves are quite rounded at the base and have three, very prominent linear veins. The delicate four-petaled flowers are a deep pink with long, distinctive, arched, yellow stamens, and are borne in a loose terminal cluster. There are ten species of this genus across North America, all preferring to grow in damp ground and all found in the east of the continent. Pale Meadow Beauty (*R. mariana*) is very similar, but its flowers are much paler and it has a smaller range.

ROSE-PINK; BITTERBLOOM
(SABATIA ANGULARIS)

Rose-pink is part of the Gentian family of leafy herbs, which is found across the world in many different habitats. Rose-pink prefers open woods and meadows and has a slender, branching stem, that is very square in section. It bears opposite pairs of small, clasping, ovate leaves and there is also a basal rosette of leaves. The pretty pink flowers are star-like and slightly sweet-scented, with five petals joined at the base, and are borne on opposite branches. The similar Saltmarsh Pink (*S. stellaris*) has pink to white flowers, more linear leaves and prefers the saline habitat of brackish meadows or coastal marshes.

FAMILY Gentian

DESCRIPTION Delicate, branching plant with a four-angled stem bearing small ovate leaves and pretty pink flowers on opposite branches

HABITAT Open woods; roadsides; meadows

HEIGHT 1–3 ft (30–90 cm)

FLOWER Radially symmetrical, ¾–1½ ins (2–3.75 cm) in diameter

FLOWERING June–September

LEAVES Ovate, clasping, up to 1 in (2.5 cm) in length

MOSS CAMPION; MOSS PINK
(SILENE ACAULIS)

As well as in the mountains of northern North America, Moss Campion is found across many areas of the Northern Hemisphere in cool alpine areas. It is a low-growing, mat-forming plant, with many short stems bearing masses of small, very narrow leaves arranged in thickly-clustered opposite pairs, mostly towards the base of the stems. The deep pink – or sometimes lilac – flowers are held on short leafy stalks just above the dense mat of leaves. The tubular calyx opens out at the end into five broad lobes that are often notched at the tip. There are around 30 species in this genus found in North America, widely spread across the continent. It is more common in the west, where plants often form a dense mat of color when they are in flower from June to August.

FAMILY Carnation
DESCRIPTION Low-growing alpine plant with small, long, thin leaves thickly clustered in opposite pairs on short branches, single small, pink to violet terminal flower
HABITAT Damp, rocky crevices above the timberline
HEIGHT 1–3 ins (2.5–7.5 cm)
FLOWER Radially symmetrical, ½ in (1.25 cm) in diameter
FLOWERING July–August
LEAVES Thin and narrow, mostly basal, up to ½ in (1.25 cm) in length

RED CLOVER
(TRIFOLIUM PRATENSE)

FAMILY Pea

DESCRIPTION Erect, hairy stem with leaves divided into three oval leaflets and with dense rounded flower heads of tiny magenta-pink flowers

HABITAT Lawns; roadsides; fields

HEIGHT 6–20 ins (15–50 cm)

FLOWER Spherical cluster, ½–1 in (1.25–2.5 cm) in width

FLOWERING May–September

LEAVES Tripalmate, each leaflet up to 2 ins (5 cm) long

Red Clover is a short, leggy perennial, with leaves divided into three oval leaflets, which often have a chevron of lighter green or white across the center. The dense, rounded flower heads are made up of 30–90 small, pea-like flowers, and are borne on erect, hairy stems. Originally from Europe, Red Clover was planted across North America as pasture for farm animals, and as a crop to make hay. It is also used in traditional crop rotation to improve the nitrogen content of the soil. Red Clover flower tea was once used as a mild sedative and for asthma and bronchitis. Extracts of Red Clover are now sold in tablet form as it is reputed to ward off cancer.

ELEGANT BRODIAEA;
(BRODIAEA ELEGANS) HARVEST BRODIAEA

The very long, narrow leaves of Elegant Brodiaea have usually totally disappeared by the time the flower comes out in late April to July. The flower ranges from purple to violet-blue in color at the tip from a greenish base and is trumpet-shaped. There are usually several flowers on each plant, held in a loose umbel cluster at the end of the bare stalk. Another very similar species, *B. coronaria*, is also commonly known as Harvest Brodiaea, but its range extends into British Columbia. There are around 37 species in this genus in North America, all found in the west half of the continent. American Indians once ate the bulbs, calling them "grass nuts."

FAMILY Lily

DESCRIPTION Loose umbel of trumpet-shaped purple to violet flowers on a leafless stalk; the long, narrow, basal leaves have withered when the plant is in flower

HABITAT Dry, stony ground

HEIGHT 4–20 ins (10–50 cm)

FLOWER Trumpet shaped, 1–1½ ins (2.5–3.75 cm) long

FLOWERING April–July

LEAVES Narrow, basal, 4–15 ins (10–37.5 cm) in length

TALL MOUNTAIN SHOOTINGSTAR
(DODECATHEON JEFFREYI)

Tall Mountain Shootingstar has the distinctive flowers of the species, with the four or five petals swept sharply back and upwards, and the stamens and stigma pointing down, creating the look of a rocket or star heading for Earth. It is very well named, as its flower stalk grows up to 24 inches (60 cm) – much higher than that of many of the other shootingstar species. The basal rosette of deep green and oblanceolate leaves are covered in tiny, glandular hairs. The bare flower stalk springs from the center of the rosette of leaves, and the red-pink to purple flowers are borne in a small to medium cluster, suspended and nodding from the top of the stalk. A perennial, Tall Mountain Shootingstar can form quite large colonies when it is growing in the right conditions. Alpine Shootingstar (*D. alpinum*) is smaller, lacks the glandular hairs on the leaves and is only found as far north as eastern Oregon.

FAMILY Primrose

DESCRIPTION Tall bare flower stalk springing from a basal rosette of deep green leaves covered in tiny glandular hairs, with a small, nodding cluster of purple flowers with backward pointing petals

HABITAT Wet mountainsides

HEIGHT 15–24 ins (37.5–60 cm)

FLOWER Radially symmetrical, ¾–1 in (2–2.5 cm) in diameter

FLOWERING June–August

LEAVES Basal rosette, oblanceolate, up to 4 ins (10 cm) long

PURPLE CONEFLOWER
(ECHINACEA PURPUREA)

FAMILY Aster

DESCRIPTION Tall perennial with long, roughly serrated leaves on long stalks, large compound flower heads with drooping purple rays and a browny-red central cone-shaped disk

HABITAT Prairies; open woodland

HEIGHT 14–50 ins (35–150 cm)

FLOWER Compound flower head, 2–4 ins (5–10 cm) in diameter

FLOWERING May–October

LEAVES Ovate, often roughly serrated, 12–24 ins (30–60 cm) long, borne on long stalks

The flowers of Purple Coneflower are used to make an herbal remedy that strengthens the immune system, and Echinacea is available as a tea, capsules, or tablets in pharmacies and health food stores across the world, so this is one wildflower that is often better known by its scientific name. Purple Coneflower is a very tall, perennial, with large, daisy-like flower heads with drooping purple, pinkish — or very rarely white — rays round a cone-shaped, browny-red central disk. The leaves are ovate, with long stalks and prominent veins, and often with serrated edges. Purple Coneflower is easy to cultivate and makes an attractive addition to the garden.

SHARP-LOBED HEPATICA
(HEPATICA NOBILIS VAR. ACUTA (ANEMONE ACUTILOBA))

There are only two species of hepatica in North America, both found in the same general area – the other is Round-lobed Hepatica (*H. nobilis var. obtusa* or *Anemone americana* – see pages 222–3). They are closely related to anemones, and some experts place them in the genus *Anemone*. Sharp-lobed Hepatica is a low-growing plant with basal leaves, each with three broadly lanceolate lobes that have distinctly pointed tips. Each plant has several slender, hairy flower stalks that terminate in a pretty, open flower with five to nine long petal-like sepals – there are no true petals. The flowers can be pale purple, lavender-blue, pink or white in color.

FAMILY Buttercup

DESCRIPTION Low-growing plant with three-lobed, pointed basal leaves, hairy stalks each bearing one lavender-blue flower

HABITAT Dry, rocky woodland

HEIGHT 4–8 ins (10–20 cm)

FLOWER Radially symmetrical, ½–1 in (1.25–2.5 cm) in diameter

FLOWERING February–June

LEAVES Basal, three-lobed, lobes lanceolate and pointed, 2–2½ins (5–6.5 cm) long

ROUND-LOBED HEPATICA; LIVERWORT

(HEPATICA NOBILIS VAR. OBTUSA (ANEMONE AMERICANA))

One of the early flowering wildflowers, Round-lobed Hepatica is a small plant with basal leaves, each of which is borne at the end of a stalk and has three rounded lobes. There are several slender, hairy flower stalks on every plant, springing from the center of the basal leaves and each ending in an attractive flower with no petals but five to nine petal-like sepals. The flowers can be pale purple, lavender-blue, pink, or white in color. Early herbalists often used this plant to treat liver ailments, hence its alternative common name of Liverwort. It was also used as an appetite stimulant and as a tonic, but it contains irritating compounds so is potentially risky to use without medical supervision. The very similar Sharp-leaved Hepatica (*H. nobilis var. acuta* or *Anemone acutiloba* — see page 221) has pointed leaf lobes.

FAMILY Buttercup

DESCRIPTION Low-growing plant with three-lobed, rounded basal leaves, hairy stalks each bearing one deep lavender-blue flower

HABITAT Dry, rocky woodland

HEIGHT 4–8 ins (10–20 cm)

FLOWER Radially symmetrical, ½–1 in (1.25–2.5 cm) in diameter

FLOWERING March–June

LEAVES Basal, three-lobed, lobes oblanceolate and rounded, 2–2½ins (5–6.5 cm) long

BLUE-POD LUPINE;
GARDEN LUPINE (LUPINUS POLYPHYLLUS)

FAMILY Pea

DESCRIPTION Stout, hollow-stemmed plant, compound palmate leaves with leaflets arranged like wheel spokes, tall dense racemes of violet or purple-blue pea-like flowers

HABITAT Damp meadows; moist forests; along streams

HEIGHT 2–5 ft (60–150 cm)

FLOWER Raceme spike, each flower ½ in (1.25 cm) long

FLOWERING June–August

LEAVES Compound palmate, with leaflets arranged like wheel spokes

There are over 150 species of lupine across the whole of North America, most of them in the west although a few do grow in the east. The seeds are a very valuable food for wild birds, but the plants themselves are poisonous to livestock. Blue-pod Lupine is one of the tallest western lupines, with stout hollow stems each bearing a dense raceme spike, 6–18 ins (15–45 cm) long, of purple to blue-violet flowers, which are rather like those of the pea. The leaves are roughly round overall, but palmately divided into 9–17 leaflets, each radiating out like the spokes of a wheel from a common central stalk. Plants spread easily, creating a mass of color when in flower.

BABY-BLUE-EYES

(NEMOPHILA MENZIESII)

Baby-blue-eyes is one of the best known wildflowers in the west. It is a low-growing plant, with long, slender branches bearing many pinnately divided leaves in opposite pairs at the end of short stalks, each segment deeply lobed. The pretty flowers are bowl-shaped, with five wide lobes that are deep purple-blue at the tip, fading to white at the base and speckled with black. Each flower is held at the end of a long, slender stalk. Baby-blue-eyes is often included in wildflower seed mixes, so it may be found outside its area. *N. phacelioides* is also known as Baby blue-eyes but has longer, more oval segmented leaves and prefers sandy, open woodland.

FAMILY Waterleaf

DESCRIPTION Low-growing, branching plant with slender branches bearing many leaves, and pretty, bowl-shaped purple-blue flowers at the end of long, slender stalks

HABITAT Open hillsides

HEIGHT 3–12 ins (8–30 cm)

FLOWER Radially symmetrical, ½–2 ins (1.25–5 cm) in diameter

FLOWERING April–June

LEAVES Pinnately divided, each segment deeply lobed, up to 2 ins (5 cm) long

SKY PILOT
(POLEMONIUM VISCOSUM)

Sky Pilot has clumps of stout stems that are covered in sticky, glandular hairs. The compound leaves are long, narrow and sessile, pinnately divided into leaflets, which are divided at the base into several tiny lobes. Each leaf is also covered in glandular hairs and both stem and leaves exude a rather unpleasant, skunk-like smell. The attractive, funnel-shaped flowers are borne at the end of the stem, with several in a very loose, rounded corymb cluster. They are usually purple-blue, but are sometimes white or yellow. Sky Pilot gets its common name because it thrives at high altitudes above the timberline, and does less well at lower levels in the mountains. Another species, Elegant Polemonium (*P. elegans*), which is found in the Cascade Ranges from Washington into British Columbia, is very similar but has leaflets that are not divided.

FAMILY Phlox

DESCRIPTION Leafy plant with clumps of stout stems all covered in short, sticky hairs and funnel-shaped violet-blue flowers in loose, rounded heads; hairs emit an unpleasant, skunk-like smell

HABITAT Open, rocky places at high altitude

HEIGHT 2–20 ins (5–50 cm)

FLOWER Radially symmetrical, ½–1 in (1.25–2.5 cm) in diameter

FLOWERING June–August

LEAVES Sessile, compound pinnate, leaflets lobed at base, 4–6 ins (10–15 cm) in length

PICKERELWEED
(PONTEDERIA CORDATA)

FAMILY Pickerelweed

DESCRIPTION Aquatic plant with heart-shaped leaves on long stems extending above the water level and small violet-blue flowers in spikes at the end of long stalks

HABITAT Freshwater marshes; shallow edges of ponds and lakes

HEIGHT 1–2 ft (30–60 cm) above the water level

FLOWER Elongated cluster, each flower ½ in (1.25 cm) long

FLOWERING July–November

LEAVES Basal, cordate, up to 10 ins (25 cm) long

Pickerelweed is an aquatic plant that grows in shallow water at the edges of ponds and lakes and in marshes. It is a stout plant with a submerged rhizome, and creeping stems that allow it to spread quickly. The basal, heart-shaped, smooth green leaves are on long stems that extend up above the water level. The flower spikes are made up of many purple to blue, funnel-shaped flowers, thickly clustered in an elongated, rounded cone. The flower has two lips, the lower lip in three parts and the upper divided into three lobes; the central lobe has two yellow spots. The young leaves of Pickerelweed can be added to salads, or cooked as a pot herb.

PURPLE MOUNTAIN SAXIFRAGE
(SAXIFRAGA OPPOSITIFOLIA)

A low-growing plant, Purple Mountain Saxifrage forms dense mats on rocky ground. Its thickly-clustered stems bear small, ovate leaves arranged in opposite pairs, mostly towards the lower part of the stem. The leaves are sometimes tinged with purple, and have hairy edges. The flowers are bright lavender-pink or purple-rose in color with one at the tip of each stem. Other species of saxifrage found in the same general area as Purple Mountain Saxifrage include White Mountain Saxifrage (*S. paniculata*), with white flowers and basal leaves, and Yellow Mountain Saxifrage (*S. aizoides*), which has very bright yellow flowers.

FAMILY Saxifrage

DESCRIPTION Low-growing plant forming dense clumps on rocky ground, with tiny oval leaves and small, bright lavender-pink flowers

HABITAT Rocks; ledges; cliffs

HEIGHT 1–4 ins (2.5–10 cm)

FLOWER Radially symmetrical, ½ in (1.25 cm) in diameter

FLOWERING June–August

LEAVES Small, ovate, hairy edges, to ¼ in (0.5 cm) long

NEW ENGLAND ASTER
(SYMPHYOTRICHUM NOVAE-ANGLIAE (ASTER NOVAE-ANGLIAE))

New England Aster is a large plant, growing up to 8 ft (240 cm) tall, with a stout, bristly-hairy, branching stem. The many long, lanceolate leaves clasp the stem and are arranged alternately at uneven intervals. The compound, daisy-like flower heads are borne mainly towards the ends of the branches in loose clusters. They have yellowish central disk florets and 40–50 ray florets that are often purple-blue, but can be white or lavender – there is also a cultivated pink variety. The narrow bracts are hairy and sticky. New England Aster is one of the best-known American asters and is often cultivated in gardens. American Indians made a tea from the roots to treat diarrhea and fevers. New York Aster (*S. novi-belgii*, or *Aster novi-belgii* – see page 232) has mostly smooth stems with smaller leaves and does not grow so high. Its central disk can be yellow or reddish. It prefers coastal areas, but parts of its range overlap.

FAMILY Aster
DESCRIPTION Large, stout hairy plant with branching stem and long, lanceolate leaves; compound, daisy-like lavender-purple flower heads in clusters at branch ends
HABITAT Wet meadows; swamps
HEIGHT 32–96 ins (80–240 cm)
FLOWER Compound flower head, 1–2 ins (2.5–5 cm) in diameter
FLOWERING August–October
LEAVES Lanceolate, clasping, up to 5 ins (12.5 cm) long

NEW YORK ASTER
(SYMPHYOTRICHUM NOVI-BELGII (ASTER NOVI-BELGII))

FAMILY Aster

DESCRIPTION Large, smooth-stemmed plant with many branches, clasping, long, lanceolate leaves and loose clusters of compound violet-blue daisy-like flowers

HABITAT Shorelines; wet meadows

HEIGHT 10–60 ins (25–150 cm)

FLOWER Compound flower head, 1–2 ins (2.5–5 cm) in diameter

FLOWERING August–October

LEAVES Lanceolate, clasping, up to 6 ins (15 cm) in length

A large plant, with a slender, smooth, branching stem, New York Aster is abundant near the coast, but is commonly found only up to 100 miles inland. It has many long, lanceolate leaves arranged alternately and partly clasping the stem. The compound daisy-like flower heads are borne mainly towards the ends of the branches, and they have yellowish or reddish central disk florets with many ray florets that are usually purple-blue, but can be white or rose-pink. The narrow bracts are greenish-white. There are many flower heads on each plant, in loose clusters towards the top, creating a splash of color when they are in flower.

BLUE VERVAIN
(VERBENA HASTATA)

Blue Vervain is an attractive plant, with its long, thin multiple flower spikes that make it look rather like a candelabrum. The square and grooved stem bears long, lanceolate, sharply and coarsely-toothed leaves arranged in opposite pairs, which have a very rough surface texture. The individual flowers open in a circle around the spike, moving upwards from the base in sequence, and are usually violet-blue in color – although rarely they can be pink. American Indians and 19th-century doctors used a medicinal tea made from the leaves as a general tonic specifically for women, and also to cure fevers and stomach complaints.

FAMILY Verbena

DESCRIPTION Tall, perennial plant with a grooved, branching stem and lanceolate leaves, many stiff flower spikes arranged rather like a candelabrum, with violet-blue flowers

HABITAT Wet woodland; damp fields

HEIGHT 2–6 ft (60–180 cm)

FLOWER Spike, each flower $\frac{1}{8}$ in (0.31 cm) in diameter

FLOWERING July–September

LEAVES Lanceolate, toothed, up to 6 ins (15 cm) long

HOARY VERVAIN
(VERBENA STRICTA)

FAMILY Verbena
DESCRIPTION Tall plant with a hairy stem, obovate toothed leaves and dense spikes of tiny purple flowers
HABITAT Dry fields
HEIGHT 2–10 ft (60–300 cm)
FLOWER Spike, each flower ½ in (1.25 cm) in length
FLOWERING June–August
LEAVES Obovate, coarsely and irregularly toothed, up to 6 ins (15 cm) long

Hoary Vervain can be quite a large plant, growing up to 10 feet (300 cm) in height, so it is quite noticeable in its chosen habitat. It is found across most of the eastern North American states, usually growing in dry fields. It has a long stem covered in a fine coating of whitish hairs — hence hoary as part of the common name — that can either be singular or branched. The sessile leaves are obovate, coarsely and irregularly toothed and arranged along the stem in opposite pairs. The purple — occasionally pink — flowers are borne in long, dense spikes, often several at the top of each plant, and they flower around the spike alternately, moving upwards.

COMMON BLUE VIOLET
(VIOLA SORORIA (VIOLA PAPILIONACEA, VIOLA FLORIDANA))

Common Blue Violet is a pretty, low-growing plant, bearing quite broad, heart-shaped leaves with scalloped edges on short stalks springing from the base of the plant. The flowers are the typical violet shape and are purple, blue, or white – there is also a pale gray form of this species, which is known as the Confederate Violet. There are usually many flowers on a plant, each with its own separate stalk springing from the base. Like many other violets, flowers low down on the plant often to not open, but they produce many seeds. Violet flowers can be candied, and the leaves are high in vitamins and can be used in salads.

FAMILY Violet
DESCRIPTION Low-growing plant with heart-shaped, scalloped leaves and purple flowers on slender stalks
HABITAT Damp woodland, moist meadows; wet roadsides
HEIGHT 4–8 ins (10–20 cm)
FLOWER Irregular with two symmetrical halves, ½–¾ in (1.25–2 cm) in diameter
FLOWERING March–May
LEAVES Cordate, scalloped, 2–5 ins (10–12.5 cm) long

COLORADO BLUE COLUMBINE
(AQUILEGIA CAERULEA (AQUILEGIA COERULEA))

Colorado Blue Columbine is Colorado's state flower. It is a very attractive bushy perennial, with several stems bearing many compound palmate leaves. The rather rounded leaflets are cleft and lobed. The flowers are very large and showy, with five pointed, petal-like sepals on the outside and five curving petals inside, each of which has a long, backward-pointing spur. The sepals are normally a bright sky blue and the petals much paler blue to white, with the spur a deeper blue, but since this species has been extensively cultivated and has also hybridized with other wildflowers there are many variations in color to be found, and also forms with double flowers. A similar but much smaller species is Alpine Blue Columbine (*A. saximontana*), which has blue spurs hooked at the tips, and grows only high in the mountains of Colorado.

FAMILY Buttercup

DESCRIPTION Many-stemmed, bushy plant with divided leaves and pretty flowers with white petals surrounded by petal-like blue sepals

HABITAT Mountains; woods at high altitude

HEIGHT 28–34 ins (70–85 cm)

FLOWER Radially symmetrical, 2–3 ins (5–8 cm) in diameter

FLOWERING July–August

LEAVES Compound palmate, leaflets cleft and lobed, each up to 1½ ins (2.5–3.75 cm) long

COMMON CAMAS
(CAMASSIA QUAMASH)

FAMILY Lily

DESCRIPTION A perennial plant growing from a bulb, with very long, narrow leaves and blue star-like flowers in an elongated raceme cluster

HABITAT Wet meadows

HEIGHT 6–32 ins (15–80 cm)

FLOWER Elongated raceme cluster, each flower 1–2 ins (2.5–5 cm) wide

FLOWERING April–June

LEAVES Linear, mostly towards the base, up to 24 ins (60 cm) long

Common Camas can be very abundant, covering an entire field with blue. It has a single stem with several long, linear, grass-like leaves springing from the base. The blue to blue-lavender star-shaped flowers grow in an elongated raceme cluster at the top of a bare stalk. A species with radially symmetrical flowers that is only found west of the Cascade Range was once classed separately as *C. leichtlinii*, but is now included in the main species. The bulbs can be cooked and eaten, but only if identification is certain as the Death Camas (*Zigadenus venenosus*), which has white or bronze flowers but is otherwise very similar, is extremely poisonous.

HAREBELL; BLUEBELL
(CAMPANULA ROTUNDIFOLIA)

This pretty wildflower is also found across Europe and Asia. It has a smooth, slender stem with sparse, linear leaves arranged alternately along the stem, and rounded, slightly heart-shaped basal leaves that appear early in the plant's development and die back before it flowers. The bell-shaped blue to violet-blue flowers have five pointed lobes that curve outwards, and are borne at the end of short stalks at the top of the plant. Flowers growing in the shade are a much more intense blue. There are 29 species in this genus found across North America, most of them with blue flowers — although there are some with white.

FAMILY Bellflower

DESCRIPTION Smooth-stemmed plant with rounded lower leaves and linear upper leaves, blue-violet bell-shaped flowers hanging at the top of a slender stalk

HABITAT Open, rocky areas at medium to high elevations

HEIGHT 6–30 ins (15–75 cm)

FLOWER Bell-shaped, ½–1 in (1.25–2.5 cm) in length

FLOWERING July–September

LEAVES Basal orbicular; stem linear and alternate, up to 3 ins (7.5 cm) long

CHICORY
(CICHORIUM INTYBUS)

A perennial herb, Chicory was introduced to North America from Eurasia and is now abundant across the continent. It is a tall plant, often growing up to 6 ft (180 cm), with rather sparse, long, partly-clasping leaves, which are toothed along the edges. The large, attractive flowers are borne directly from the upper parts of the main branches. The flowers are usually a clear blue-violet – although occasionally a white- or pink-flowered form appears. The blunt ends of the petals have fine, sharp teeth and the flowers do not last long in the sunshine, usually wilting by midday. The long tap root of Chicory can be roasted and the plant is often grown for its roots, which can be used as a substitute for coffee. The young, tender leaves can be used in salads, or cooked as greens. Chicory grows on areas of waste ground more or less everywhere, but it does much better in areas with lots of rain.

FAMILY Aster
DESCRIPTION Branching plant, with sparse upper leaves and pale blue flower heads with toothed petals, milky sap
HABITAT Roadsides; waste ground; field borders
HEIGHT 1–6 ft (30–180 cm)
FLOWER Radially symmetrical, 2 ins (5 cm) in diameter
FLOWERING April–October
LEAVES Lanceolate, toothed or lobed, up to 10 ins (25 cm) in length

ERECT DAYFLOWER;
SLENDER DAYFLOWER (COMMELINA ERECTA)

FAMILY Spiderwort

DESCRIPTION Variable plant, but often erect and branching, with long, lanceolate, sheathing leaves and blue flowers with two large rounded petals and one tiny

HABITAT Sandy or rocky soil; open woods; overgrown ground

HEIGHT 14 ins (35 cm)

FLOWER Irregular with two symmetrical halves, 1 in (2.5 cm) in diameter

FLOWERING May–September

LEAVES Lanceolate, narrow, sheathing, up to 6 ins (15 cm) in length

Erect Dayflower is variable in appearance but is usually a small perennial with some erect stems and a few trailing ones that root at the leaf nodes. The long, narrow leaves sheath the stems, and the flowers are borne in small clusters at the top of the plant. They have two large, broad upper blue petals and one smaller whitish lower one, and each flower blooms for only one day, hence the common name. There are eight species of dayflower found in the United States, all very similar in appearance and all found in the southwest. Asiatic Dayflower (*C. Communis*) has been introduced from Asia, and is a troublesome weed in many areas.

CLOSED BOTTLE GENTIAN
(GENTIANA ANDREWSII)

The Closed Bottle Gentian is one of the most widespread gentians in North America. It has bottle-shaped, bright blue flowers arranged in a tight, rounded cluster on its stem – usually in the axil of a whorl of smooth, ovate to lanceolate leaves. At the tip of the flower the petals are very slightly open, showing fringed edges between the lobes. The stem also has leaves arranged in opposite pairs lower down. Other similar species include Blind Gentian (*G. clausa*), which is almost identical except that the petals are tightly closed at the tip of the flower, and Narrow-leaved Gentian (*G. linearis*), in which the flowers are more open and the leaves narrower.

FAMILY Gentian

DESCRIPTION Medium-size plant with ovate to lanceolate leaves in opposite pairs on stem, whorled below the dark blue, bottle-shaped, tight cluster of flowers

HABITAT Damp meadows; wet thickets

HEIGHT 1–2 ft (30–60 cm)

FLOWER Tight, rounded cluster, each flower 1–1½ ins (2.5–3.75 cm) long

FLOWERING August–October

LEAVES Ovate to lanceolate, opposite; whorled below the flower cluster, up to 4 ins (10 cm)

HARVESTBELLS;
SOAPWORT GENTIAN (GENTIANA SAPONARIA)

FAMILY Gentian

DESCRIPTION Medium-size plant with ovate to lanceolate leaves in opposite pairs on stem, whorled below the light blue, bottle-shaped, tight cluster of flowers

HABITAT Damp meadows; wet thickets

HEIGHT 1–2 ft (30–60 cm)

FLOWER Tight, rounded cluster, each flower 1–1½ ins (2.5–3.75 cm) in length

FLOWERING August–October

LEAVES Ovate to lanceolate, opposite; whorled below flower cluster, up to 4 ins (10 cm) long

Harvestbells has bottle-shaped flowers, with the tip slightly open, arranged in a tight, rounded cluster, usually in the axil of a whorl of smooth, ovate to lanceolate leaves. It looks extremely similar to Closed Bottle Gentian (*G. andrewsii* – see page 243) and Blind Gentian (*G. clausa*) except its flowers are pale blue. As well as the whorl beneath the flowers, the stem has further leaves arranged in opposite pairs lower down. Another common name for Harvestbells is Soapwort Gentian, because of its soapy-looking sap. It is found further west than the other two common species, but prefers the same kind of damp habitat in meadows and open thickets.

AZURE BLUET;
QUAKER LADIES;INNOCENCE
(HOUSTONIA CAERULEA (HEDYOTIS CAERULEA))

A delicate and petite plant, Azure Bluet prefers to grow in acid soil in small colonies, where it carpets the ground in pale blue when it flowers. The flowers are borne at the tip of long, slender stalks, three or four to a plant rising from a basal cluster of leaves. The stalks also have tiny leaves arranged in opposite pairs at intervals. The flowers have four petals in delicate pale blue or violet-blue, fading to white at the center and with a bright yellow central disk. Cherokee Indians used a tea made from the leaves to stop bed-wetting. There are 30 species of bluet across North America, but none of them grows wild in the northwest.

FAMILY Madder

DESCRIPTION Low-growing plant with small oblong basal leaves and tiny opposite stem leaves, pale blue flowers on slender erect stems

HABITAT Grassy fields; lawns; open woodland

HEIGHT 3–6 ins (7.5–15 cm)

FLOWER Radially symmetrical, ½ in (1.25 cm) in diameter

FLOWERING April–June

LEAVES Basal oblong, ½ in (1.25 cm) long; upper small and opposite

GREAT LOBELIA;
BLUE CARDINAL FLOWER
(LOBELIA SIPHILITICA)

FAMILY Bellflower

DESCRIPTION Tall perennial with oval to lanceolate leaves and a long spike of bright blue flowers

HABITAT Damp woodland; swamps; moist meadows

HEIGHT 2–5 ft (60–150 cm)

FLOWER Spike, each flower 1 in (2.5 cm) in length

FLOWERING August–October

LEAVES Oval to lanceolate, sometimes toothed, 2–6 ins (5–15 cm) long

Great Lobelia is a tall perennial, with a spike of flowers that can be 1–2 feet (30–60 cm) long at the top of a leafy stem. The flowers are unusual, with three lobes at the bottom and two above; the underneath of the lower part is striped in white. The long leaves are oval or lanceolate and sometimes coarsely toothed along the edges. American Indians used a tea made from the roots to treat syphilis – hence its scientific name – and a tea of the leaves for colds, fevers, and stomach problems. However, the plant is potentially poisonous. Cardinal Flower (*L. cardinalis* – see page 30) is almost identical to Great Lobelia, except its flowers are red.

WILD LUPINE
(LUPINUS PERENNIS)

Wild Lupine is a tall, erect plant with a brownish, branched stem, bearing palmate leaves with seven to eleven leaflets arranged like the spokes of a wheel. Further south in its range, a form with narrower leaflets is known as Nuttall's Lupine (*L. Nuttallii*). The tall, showy raceme is made up of pea-like flowers are arranged in whorls on the stalk. The flowers are usually blue and white, but the blue may be quite violet. American Indians used a cold tea made from the leaves to treat nausea and internal hemorrhaging. Miniature Lupine (*L. bicolor*) is a similar but much smaller plant and is found in the west, not the east.

FAMILY Pea

DESCRIPTION Erect-stemmed plant with palmate leaves, the leaflets like the spokes of a wheel, and a long upright terminal cluster of pea-like blue flowers

HABITAT Dry open fields; woods

HEIGHT 9–28 ins (22–70 cm)

FLOWER Raceme, each flower ¾ in (2 cm) long

FLOWERING April–July

LEAVES Palmate, with leaflets like wheel spokes from a central stalk, each leaflet up to 2 ins (5 cm) long

MOUNTAIN BLUEBELLS
(MERTENSIA CILIATA)

Mountain Bluebells is not necessarily found at high altitudes despite its name — it prefers wet and boggy ground and is often found growing along streams or seeps. It is a tall plant — often growing up to 40 ins (100 cm) — and tends to grow in clumps, with several long, leafy stems. The bright green leaves are elliptical, those towards the base of the plant with long stalks, and are arranged alternately on the stem. At the tip of the stems are loose, drooping cyme clusters of blue, narrowly bell-shaped flowers. As they age, the flowers turn pink-red, so there are often two colors of flower in the same cluster at one time. Plants in this genus are often also known as lungwort, as in Europe there is a species that was once believed to be a cure for diseases of the lung. Mountain Bluebells is found through most of the mid-western states, from central Oregon and down as far south as northern New Mexico.

FAMILY Borage

DESCRIPTION Leafy-stemmed plant growing in clumps, with long, elliptical leaves and a loose cyme cluster of narrow, bell-shaped blue-pink flowers

HABITAT Wet meadows; seeps; along streams

HEIGHT 8–40 ins (20–100 cm)

FLOWER Loose cyme cluster, each flower ½–¾ in (1.25–2 cm) wide

FLOWERING May–July

LEAVES Elliptical, long-stalked, up to 6 ins (15 cm) long

AMERICAN PASQUEFLOWER
(PULSATILLA PATENS (ANEMONE PATENS))

FAMILY Buttercup

DESCRIPTION Small, very hairy-stemmed plant, with small basal leaves and a whorl of narrowly-segmented, crowed leaves beneath the bowl-shaped blue flower

HABITAT Prairies; plains; open wasteland

HEIGHT 8–16 ins (20–40 cm)

FLOWER Radially symmetrical, 2½ ins (6.25 cm) in diameter

FLOWERING April–May

LEAVES Basal, compound palmate; stem, sessile, linear, segmented, up to 4 ins (10 cm) long, whorled just beneath flower

Pasque is a corruption of the French word Pâques, meaning Easter, which is roughly when this plant flowers. The basal leaves of American Pasqueflower are hairy and compound palmate, with the leaflets deeply divided into narrow segments. Higher up the stem, just beneath the flowers, three smaller, hairy, sessile leaves are divided into linear lobes. The several stems are softly hairy, and terminate in solitary, bowl-shaped flowers with five to seven blue, violet, or white petal-like sepals, but no petals. The seeds of American Pasqueflower are quite distinctive, as they are each tipped with a long tail that creates a feathery-looking seed head.

BLUE-EYED GRASS
(SISYRINCHIUM ANGUSTIFOLIUM)

Even experts disagree on whether some of the variants of Blue-eyed Grass are separate species or not, so is difficult to make an identification with any certainty. It is a medium-size plant with long, linear, rather grass-like leaves in a cluster at the base, although it is not related to true grasses. The attractive flowers are borne at the end of a long, flat stem – there are usually two but with only one in bloom at any one time. The six petal-like segments open out widely at the ends, and are blue to blue-violet. They are notched twice at the tip, with a longer, central point. Blue-eyed Grass grows in fields and meadows across most of North America.

FAMILY Iris
DESCRIPTION Plant with long, linear, grass-like leaves and a flat stem bearing one or two delicate blue flowers with broad notched and pointed petal-like segments
HABITAT Fields; meadows
HEIGHT 6–20 ins (15–50 cm)
FLOWER Radially symmetrical, ½ in (1.25 cm) in diameter
FLOWERING May–July
LEAVES Basal, linear, grass-like

INDEX OF COMMON NAMES

INDEX OF SCIENTIFIC NAMES

PICTURE CREDITS

The publisher would like to thank Photolibrary.com for providing the photographs for this book. We would also like to thank the following for their kind permission to reproduce their photographs:

Adam Jones 29, 231; Anthony Nyssen/SAL 241; B. G. Murray, Jr/AA 235; Bill Beaty/AA 81, 127, 130, 151, 245; Bob Gibbons 25, 70, 72, 147, 163, 216; Breck P Kent/AA 91, 209, 237; Brian Milne/AA 229; Bruce M Wellman/AA 213; Bruce McDonald/AA 162; C. C. Lockwood/AA 128; Carroll W Perkins/AA 40, 145; Charles Palek/AA 55; Daniel Cox 215; David Cayless 232; David Fox 105; David M Dennis 39, 115; David Wriggelsworth 228, 247; Daybreak Imagery 83, 87; Deni Bown 58, 69, 85, 99, 104, 108, 109, 135, 144, 152, 155, 169, 177, 220, 246; Dominique Braud/AA 41; Don Enger/AA 148; Donald Specker/AA 93, 138, 187; Doug Wechsler/AA 143; Duncan Murell 79; E. R. Degginger/AA 35, 48, 94, 198; Fred Whitehead/AA 77; Geoff Kidd 67, 101, 112, 184; George E. Sawyer/AA 160; Gordon Maclean 57, 118, 131, 178, 205; Harry Engels/AA 54; Harry Fox 45, 80, 125; Heikki Nikki 250; Ian West 76, 224; Jack Wilburn/AA 111, 204, 217; Jack Wilburn/Earth Sciences 73; Joanne F Huemoeller/AA 100, 251; Joe McDonald/AA 36; John Anderson/AA 242; John C Stevenson/AA 201; John Cooke 191; John Gerlach/AA 33, 133, 171, 183, 219, 225; John Lemkar/AA 113, 120, 168, 189; John Mitchell 117; Joyce & Frank Burek/Earth Sciences 140; M. W. Endler 114; Malcolm Coe 197; Marcia W. Grifffen 185; Maresa Pryor/Earth Sciences 165; Mark Hamblin 137; Michael Gadomski 43, 149; Michael Gadomski/AA 43, 62, 179; Mills Tandy 47, 50, 66, 186, 206, 210; Niall Benvie 239; Osf 51, 103, 119, 129, 159; Patti Murray/AA 95, 136, 141, 174, 227, 249; Perry D. Slocum/AA 161, 170, 244; Peter Clark/SAL 167; Peter Gathercole 96; Rich Reid/AA 31; Richard Day/AA 202; Richard Kolar 30, 53, 63, 181, 203, 206, 243; Richard Shiell/AA 49, 123, 158, 190. 233, 234; Robert A. Lubeck/AA 59, 97; Stan Osilinski 44, 75, 84, 139, 153, 166, 193; Steffen Hauser 90; Stephen Ingram/AA 89, 107; Ted Levin/AA 61, 194; Tom Leach 26, 175; Waina Cheng 65, 121; Wendy Neefus/AA 157; Zig Leszczynki/AA 32, 88, 71, 212;

With thanks to Simon Pittaway and Kate Truman.
Main cover image: joSon/Getty Images